Belongs To Agel. Tand.
Budappy Uni

品 an item of food. An ingredient. Composed of three ideograms for 'mouth' 口, it also shows the movement of the mouth when chewing food. In Chinese culture, table settings for three dishes, and the arrangement of three items of food on a plate, are always in the form of this character 品. It is the accepted, refined way to present Chinese food.

Secrets of
CHINESE
NUTRITION

168 Traditional, Delicious & Health-giving Recipes

Ng Siong Mui

◦LANDM△RK◦BOOKS◦

The recipes in this cookery book are marked with symbols to indicate if they have yin ●, yang ○, or neutral ◖properties. Those without symbols are helpful to specific common conditions as indicated in the anecdotes. To obtain full benefit from the recipes, please refer to the *Introduction* of the text.

ALL RECIPES IN THIS BOOK SERVE 4.

Originally published as *Secrets of Nutritional Chinese Cookery* in 1988
This revised edition, published 2014

Text copyright © 2011 Sandy Chui
Photography copyright © 2014 Ee Kay Gie

Illustrations by Lim Tiong Ghee

All rights reserved. No part of this publication may be reproduced or transmitted in any form or by any means, electronic or mechanical, including photocopy, recording or any information storage and retrieval system, without prior permission in writing from the publisher.

Published by
Landmark Books Pte Ltd
5001 Beach Road,
02-73/74
Singapore 199588

Landmark Books is an imprint of Landmark Books Pte Ltd

ISBN 978-981-4189-23-1

Printed in Singapore

CONTENTS

INTRODUCTION

I was born into a family of food lovers. Yes, I mean the real thing: delicious, nutritious and irresistible food. And for generations, my family has been in the business of food and food products.

Grandfather's roots were in the Village of the Heavenly Stream 天河 by the River's Gate 江门 in Sun Wui, Canton. There, he sold rice and provisions till, like many of his generation, the pressures of social unrest pushed him to emigrate and start a new life. He fled to Singapore with his wife and two children in the 1920s, and to support the family, my grandparents became itinerant hawkers, plying the streets selling their best home-cooked noodles and congee.

My father helped at the store and became fascinated with food preparation and cooking. This fascination never left him, and throughout his life, he continued to experiment in the kitchen, drawing inspiration from the Chinese culinary texts which he loved to read.

Grandfather unfortunately died after the Second World War, six months after my birth. At that time, Father struck out on his own and established Chew Kee Restaurant. It was a time of great promise and I was considered my father's lucky star. Father appointed himself principal cook of his restaurant and as business flourished, he found six cooks from China to assist him. They were specialists in their own right and among them were a noodle maker, a cutter, a spicy stew specialist and a kitchen coordinator.

Even though life was so much better than before, Grandmother would not be idle. Instead, she continued to sell her famous fish head noodles in the evening as a hobby of sorts. Mother, on her part, was busy having babies, and soon she gave me a sister and three brothers.

Each of us had our own Cantonese amah who strove to outshine each other in caring for us. In particular, they were always in the kitchen simmering a soup or double-boiling a tonic for one of us. "You look pale today, eat this. It is such hot weather these days, drink that," we'd be told. We always obeyed and didn't mind in the least because everything was delicious!

Father started training us to follow his footsteps at a young age. Suppertime was accompanied by Chinese legends and narratives on Chinese food culture, and by the time I was twelve, I was already able to help him plan a new menu for the restaurant. With such a rich culinary heritage, it was not a suprise that I chose to major in Home Economics in school.

My love for cookery deepened again after my marriage, but this time, it was with bitter food since my husband is a herbalist! His journals and reference books fascinated me and I began researching the properties of different herbs and how they colour the taste and nutritional values of various foods. I also became interested in the study of body constitutions according to ancient Chinese principles. This was in 1973. Since then, my husband and I have made numerous trips to China, meeting other herbalists and learning the secrets of Chinese health concepts.

Friends and relatives began consulting me on Chinese food therapy. "What should I eat for this dry, hacking cough?" "My children are having exams. What tonic can I brew for them?" "What food can I prepare for my in-law who is recuperating from an operation?" These were typical of the questions which came my way, and I found I had the answers.

Through the years, my research has opened up for me the mysteries of Chinese nutritional health concepts. Let me share some of their secrets with you.

The Chou dynasty *Book of Rites* record that over four thousand years ago, the ancestors of the Chinese race, personified as Fu Hsi, observed the opposing forces of nature and developed the concept of 'yin' and 'yang', the balance between conflicting elements which keep the universe in harmony. This idea was extended to food by another group of pre-historic Chinese people given the persona of Shen Nung by Han scholars. The father of agriculture and the patron saint of herbal medicne, Shen Nung, by tasting and eating the herbs in the fields and forests, discovered the medical and nutritional use of grains, nuts and herbs. But, according to the scholars of the Warring States (475 – 221 B.C.), it was Huang Ti or the Yellow Emperor (2698 – 2589 B.C), who first formulated the concept of food therapy: that the way to maintain good health is by eating the right choice of food.

The Chinese have always seen Man as part of Nature and from this belief sprung a body of code words which has no equivalent in any other language.

'Yin', the negative, dark force of nature. Pale persons with slow blood circulation who suffer from cold spells and fall ill easily are typical of people with 'yin' body complex.

'Yang', the positive, active force lies at the opposing end of the scale. Typical of a 'yang' body complex are active persons who perspire easily and have a rosy complexion.

'Wind' is the suddent movement of the body's internal energy which may manifest itself in unpleasant sensations like aches and pains, rashes and even migraine attacks.

'Damp' is the retention of fluid in the body resulting in swelling at the joints, while 'dryness' is the lack of fluids and oils which, superficially, may cause dry skin, brittle hair and chapped lips.

As in the physical world, where harmony in nature brings about peaceful conditions, the principles of Chinese food therapy state that health is the result of harmony within the body. It is only when one's body complex is at a balance or is 'neutral' that one is considered healthy. To obtain and maintain that state, the traditional Chinese eats foods opposing his body complex to achieve harmony within his body.

This follows that foods too, can be classified as 'yin' (cooling) or 'yang' (heaty). In the Ming dynasty (1518 – 1593), Li Shih Chen spent 28 years compiling his famous tome in which he classified all edible vegetable, animal and mineral products. He not only recorded the findings of centuries of empirical study determining whether an ingredient is 'yin', 'yang' or 'neutral', he also classified ingredients according to their use. Li listed all nutritious foods as 'superior items', those used for medication as 'standard items' and poisonous substances used by physicians for medical benefit as 'lower items'. Following this classification, it is the basic tenet of Chinese nutritional food therapy that 'superior items' should be eaten to balance one's body complex.

Beyond this basic premise is the need to consider the effect of weather, the activity level of the person and the method used to cook food when attempting to achieve a 'neutral' body complex.

Take a busy business executive for instance. He is a 'yang' person. After a rainy and boring day of paperwork, he comes home for dinner. His meal should be 'neutral' steamed food and a simmered soup since his 'yang' elements would already have been neutralised by his quiet day. However, if the same executive has had a hot, stressful day, he should be given 'cooling' or 'yin' food prepared by steaming, simmering or lightly oiled stir-frying to balance the 'yang' elements in his system.

In preparing this book, I have organised the recipes under different methods of healthy cooking (note that the deep-frying method has been omitted). The use of strong herbs and recipes which have medicinal values have also been excluded, and most recipes use nutritional 'superior items'.

And while I have included a number of helpful receipes which benefit particular age groups or those with specific common conditions, all the recipes produce delicious and healthy food which are suitable for every member of your household. None of the food prepared from the recipes will harm you. At best, they will relieve you of particular conditions, and at the very least, they will make a hearty and healthy meal.

I have, in the tradition of my grandfather and father, also included with each recipe, interesting information about the properties of both the main ingredient and dish. At times, I have shared personal anecdotes or given the cultural background of the dish.

Besides introducing Chinese food therapy to those unfamiliar with it, it is also my hope that this book will revive the age-old tradition of healthy eating the Chinese way. This 'yin-yang' Chinese food therapy has always been practiced as the mainstream of traditional Chinese health management. In a nutshell, food is eaten not just to fuel the body, but to please the palate and satisfy the soul. It is eaten to promote good health and prevent illness.

I have always felt that although many young Chinese do not articulate it, they still relate with, and subscribe to, the basic principles of food therapy. This is the book for them: a practical guide to eating nutritious food and maintaining good health the Chinese way.

Ng Siong Mui, 1988

STIR FRYING

炒
菜
秘
訣

To master stir frying is to master chinese cooking

Most people associate stir frying with Chinese cooking, and they are right to do so since it has been said that to master stir frying is to master Chinese cooking. The technique sounds easy – just heat the wok, throw in all the ingredients and give them a few quick stirs and that's stir frying. Indeed, that is what the Chinese character for stir frying 炒 indicates. The character has 'fire' 火 on the left and 'a little' 少 on the right, together signifying that stir frying is to use 'high heat to fry for a little while.'

However, it is not as easy as it sounds. There is an art even in this simple method. I remember that when my father tested the apprentices in his restaurant, it was never with fancy stews or roasts, but always with stir-fried greens. Whether an aspiring chef made the grade depended solely on his mastery of this technique.

Stir frying is popular because the actual cooking time averages only about five minutes, but to serve a truly satisfying stir-fried dish, time and effort must be put into the preparation of the ingredients. The colours 色, aromas 香, tastes 味 and shapes 形 of the ingredients, as well as the total effect 相 of the dish must be carefully coordinated. The short cooking time, in its part, seals in the juices of meats and keeps vegetables crisp. This retains the nutritional value of each ingredient, making them easily digestible while preserving the textures and colours of the food for a good presentation. To present an attractive and tasty stir-fried dish, four points must be observed:

First, know the nature of your ingredients. Be aware of the textural and colour combinations of ingredients used in a dish. They should be pleasing to the eye and provide variety to the palate. All ingredients must be fresh, for the fresher the ingredients, the less cooking time is required.

Second, prepare the ingredients carefully. Once the ingredients have been selected, they must be carefully measured, cleaned, soaked, drained, cut, seasoned, or even parboiled before the stir frying process begins. Different ingredients are sliced, diced or shredded to give a variety of textures and shapes. Meat is sliced thinly and across the grain. As a guide, pork should be cut into 0.2 cm (¹⁄₁₆ inch) slices while poultry and beef into 0.4 cm (⅛ inch) slices. Remember that the thinner the slices, the shorter the cooking time required.

Third, have all the seasonings and condiments required within reach. Once cooking begins, there is no time to dash around looking for this seasoning and that. The more common seasonings used include salt, sugar, pepper, corn or peanut oil, sesame oil, soya sauce and Chinese rice wine. Condiments include garlic, shallots, ginger root, spring onions, fermented black beans, brown bean sauce and chillies. These must either be finely sliced or pounded. Stock, if necessary, must also be well-prepared and strained.

Fourth, the basic rules of stir frying must be carefully followed. Prepare and rinse all the ingredients and drain well (especially for seafood and vegetables), since when water comes into contact with hot oil, the water will lower the cooking temperature and cause the oil to spatter. Sort all the ingredients according to texture and cooking time. Hard vegetables (e.g. stems of leafy vegetables, carrots, cauliflower) belong in one group and soft vegetables (e.g. leafy vegetables, snow peas and beansprouts) belong to another. This principle also applies to meat, which is determined by type and how they are cut.

This need to sort ingredients is important because they must be put into the wok in the order of their cooking times. Ingredients which require the longest cooking time are stir-fried first with the fastest cooking ingredients added last of all. This rule is to ensure that all the ingredients are evenly cooked at the end of the short cooking period. Thus, chunky ingredients (shrimps) are fried before thinly sliced ones (sliced fish fillets) and hard vegetables are cooked before soft vegetables. Never overcook vegetables as they will turn soggy and discolour.

The process of stir frying begins with what is known by the Chinese as 'exploding for fragrance' 爆香. Heat the wok till it is smoking, then add a little oil to prevent the food from sticking to the wok. Aromatic ingredients like shredded ginger, chopped shallots or garlic are then added to flavour the oil. Add the main ingredients according to their required cooking time, starting with those that need the longest time. The heat of the wok must also be controlled. Too high a heat combined with slow frying will result in a burnt dish. Insufficient heat plus overcooking will produce a soggy one.

The success of a stir-fried dish therefore lies in the coordination of several key factors. These are the basic preparation, the sequence of adding ingredients into the wok, the use of correct seasoning to enhance flavour, the perfect control of heat, and split-second timing during cooking. There are four variations of this basic stir frying technique.

SIMPLE STIR FRYING 清炒

Heat the wok with 1 tablespoon of oil. When the oil is smoking, add the condiments and fry till fragrant. Add ingredients and fry briskly for a minute or two. At times, small amounts of stock or water are added while stir frying. This should be poured in from the side of the wok so that the liquid is heated up before it mixes with the ingredients. When the ingredients are evenly cooked, dish up and serve. (See Stir-fried Mustard Greens, pg 35)

RAW STIR FRYING 生炒

Heat a wok and add a little oil when it begins to smoke. Include condiments and fry till fragrant. Put in the ingredients that require the longest cooking time and fry till they are half cooked, then add other ingredients according to their cooking times so that all the ingredients will be just done at the same time. When the last main ingredient has been put in, add the seasoning and continue to stir fry, mixing the ingredients so that they absorb the seasoning. Unlike stock or water, sauces and other seasonings are poured onto the bottom of the wok after making a well in the ingredients. This is to help ensure that seasonings are well mixed into the ingredients. When the ingredients are done and the seasoning has been absorbed, dish out and serve. (See Stir-fried Kale with Fish Fillet, pg 57)

DRY STIR FRYING 干炒

This method involves mixing all the ingredients and seasoning and stir frying them all at once. Drain water and excess marinade or seasoning from the ingredients. Heat a wok till it is very hot then put in a little oil. When the oil is smoking, add all the pre-mixed ingredients and lower the heat. Fry till the dish is done, adding oil gradually when necessary during the stir frying process. (See Scrambled Shark's Fins, Crab Meat and Eggs, pg 37)

PARBOILED STIR FRYING 熟炒

This method involves pre-cooking the ingredients separately before combining them during the stir frying process. Meats are seasoned and deep fried in very hot oil for a short time to seal in the juices 过油, (literally, to pass through oil). Vegetables, however, are parboiled 拖水, (literally, to pull through water). For a better flavour, steamed and other cooked ingredients should be cut into smaller pieces before stir frying. Also, drain the pre-cooked ingredients well before stir frying. If the same wok is used to pre-cook meats by deep frying and for the stir frying process, make sure that the wok is thoroughly cleaned before it is used for stir frying. Heat the wok till hot and add a little oil. When the oil is smoky, add the pre-cooked ingredients to stir fry quickly over high heat. Flavour with seasoning and a little sauce. Stir to mix well, dish up and serve. (See Sweet Sour Pork, pg 27)

KITCHENWARE

Wok
Wok spatula
Strainer
Colander
Pot holder

INGREDIENTS SUITABLE FOR STIR FRYING

SEAFOOD	VEGETABLES	MISCELLANEOUS	MEAT
Fish	Beansprout	Wood fungus	Pork
Shrimp	Celery	Snow fungus	Chicken
Squid	Spanish onion	Mushroom	Beef
Steamed crab meat	Carrots	Cashew nut	Liver
Shark's fin	Capsicum		Kidney
	Chilli		Giblet
	Snow pea		

TEMPERATURE AND COOKING TIMES

METHOD	PREPARATION	COOKING	TEMPERATURE
Simple Stir frying	10 minutes	2 minutes	High Heat
Raw Stir frying	15 minutes	5 minutes	High Heat
Dry Stir frying	30 minutes	5 minutes	High Heat
Parboiled Stir frying	45 minutes	5 minutes	High Heat

新年米粉

NEW YEAR FRIED VERMICELLI

400 g (14 oz) rice vermicelli
2 carrots (approx 400 g, 14 oz), skinned and shredded
400 g (14 oz) French beans, deveined and shredded
400 g (14 oz) beansprouts, roots removed
10 dried Chinese mushrooms
6 slices old ginger
3 shallots, sliced
8 tablespoons oil
1½ teaspoons salt
1½ teaspoons sugar
1½ teaspoons light soya sauce
½ tablespoon salt in 6 tablespoons water

GARNISH
10 g (0.3 oz) white sesame seeds
30 g (1 oz) sweet dried beancurd strips (*teem chok*)
1 red chilli, deseeded and shredded finely

Chinese New Year is the time when numerous friends and relatives come to visit, and Mother always chose simple, yet auspicious dishes to serve the guests. And because many of them were Buddhists, fried vegetarian rice vermicelli would be one of the dishes she prepared.

Rice vermicelli is used here because egg noodles are not eaten by orthodox Buddhists. Similarly, where ginger and shallots are permissible garnishes, coriander, chives and garlic, being mild stimulants, are taboo.

It is important to the Chinese that one's rice bowl should always be full, so rice vermicelli, being made of rice, is a great favourite. Also, the long strands of vermicelli signify longevity and is an auspicious food for the new year.

Soak rice vermicelli in warm water for 30 minutes. Drain and cut into shorter lengths. Fry the white sesame seeds over low heat without oil till golden brown. Cool and set aside. Clean and shred the sweet dried beancurd strips ½ cm crosswise. Deep fry in hot oil for 2 minutes until crispy. Drain excess oil. Cool and keep aside for garnishing.

Trim off stems and soak dried mushrooms in 175 ml (¾ cups) warm water for 30 minutes. Rinse and squeeze off excess water. Reserve mushroom water. Slice cleaned mushrooms into coarse strips.

Fry sliced mushrooms without oil over low heat for 3 minutes. Keep aside for later use.

Heat 2 tablespoons of oil in a wok. When smoking, add 2 slices ginger, 1 of the sliced shallots and fry till fragrant. Add French beans and fry for 2 minutes. Add ½ teaspoon each of salt, sugar and light soya sauce. Fry for 3 minutes. Dish out and keep aside for later use. Repeat for carrots and beansprouts. (Beansprouts require only 2 minutes cooking time).

Heat 2 tablespoons of oil in a wok. Add drained rice vermicelli and fry for 2 minutes. Add salt solution and mushroom water. Cover wok and cook rice vermicelli over medium heat for 5 minutes.

Remove wok cover, stir rice vermicelli and add fried French beans and carrots. Mix well. Now add fried beansprouts and mix well again.

Transfer fried vermicelli onto a serving dish and garnish with sweet dried beancurd strips, sesame seeds and sliced red chilli. Serve.

蝦球炒什菜 ☯

STIR-FRIED PRAWNS WITH MIXED VEGETABLES

Though prawns possess 'yang' forces, they are combined with 'yin' vegetables to produce this refreshingly 'neutral' dish. This is one of the dishes which I enjoy serving when I entertain friends.

300 g (10.5 oz) prawns, shelled and deveined
½ small carrot, skinned and sliced
100 g (3.5 oz) broccoli, cut into florets
100 g (3.5 oz) baby corn, cut into halves lengthwise
100 g (3.5 oz) beansprouts, roots removed
4 dried Chinese mushrooms, without stems, soaked and halved
4 water chestnuts, peeled and sliced
1 clove garlic, sliced
1 shallot, sliced
2 slices old ginger
750 ml (3 cups) oil

MARINADE FOR PRAWNS
1 teaspoon salt
1 teaspoon sugar
1 teaspoon light soya sauce
½ egg white
1 teaspoon cornflour
1 tablespoon oil

SEASONING
1 teaspoon salt
1 teaspoon sugar
½ teaspoon light soya sauce
½ tablespoon oyster sauce

FOR BLANCHING VEGETABLES
1 teaspoon salt
1 tablespoon oil
750 ml (3 cups) water

Dry the prawns with kitchen towels and marinate for 10 minutes. Bring the blanching solution to a boil. Blanch carrot, broccoli and baby corn separately in this water for 1 minute. Drain vegetables.

Heat 750 ml (3 cups) oil in wok until hot. Cook the marinated prawns in the hot oil for 30 seconds. Remove and drain.

Pour away the oil, leaving about 1 tablespoon. Reheat the wok, and when hot, add half the ginger and all the beansprouts. Fry for 1 minute. Ladle and set aside.

Reheat wok with 1 tablespoon oil and when smoky, add in the garlic, shallot and the remaining ginger to fry till fragrant. Add in the mushrooms, fry for 1 minute and then put in the prawns. Fry and mix well for 30 seconds.

Now, include the water chestnuts and all the blanched vegetables and seasoning. Fry well for 1 minute. Lastly, put in the sautéed beansprouts and mix thoroughly. Serve immediately.

STIR-FRIED BEANSPROUTS WITH ROAST DUCK

銀芽炒鴨絲 ◖

Blanched Chinese chives are not chives which have been pre-cooked.

They are actually Chinese chives which have been grown virtually without light. In fact, Grandmother once told me that her friend once cultivated blanched Chinese chives under her bed!

Whichever dark spot you choose, it is the lack of light which results in the plant not being able to produce chlorophyll and accounts for the blanched yellow appearance of this chive.

Because they are grown in the dark, blanched Chinese chives are a 'yin' ingredient. Combined with the 'yang' elements of roasted duck, they create a harmoniously balanced dish.

Blanched Chinese chives have a stronger taste and are more tender than ordinary chives. They are also more costly as they are considered to be a superior vegetable.

200 g (7 oz) shredded roasted duck meat
200 g (7 oz) beansprouts, roots removed
50 g (1.75 oz) blanched Chinese chives (gau wong),
    cut into 5 cm (2 inch) lengths
20 g (0.7 oz) spring onion, cut into 5 cm (2 inch) lengths
1 clove garlic, sliced
2 slices old ginger, shredded
2 tablespoons oil

SEASONING
1 teaspoon salt
1 teaspoon sugar
1 teaspoon light soya sauce

Heat a wok till hot, then put in 1 tablespoon oil and fry half the garlic and ginger till fragrant. Add in the beansprouts and chives and fry briskly for 1 minute. Ladle out and set aside.

Reheat wok with the remaining oil and fry the remaining garlic and ginger. When fragrant, add the shredded duck meat and fry well for 1 minute.

Include the cooked beansprouts, chives and spring onions. Put in the seasoning and stir well for 30 seconds. Serve immediately.

金菇炒海鮮 ☯

GOLDEN MUSHROOMS WITH SEAFOOD

400 g (14 oz) fresh golden mushrooms
1 small carrot, skinned, grated coarsely
200 g (7 oz) French beans, deveined and shredded
50 g (1.75 oz) fresh button mushrooms, sliced
50 g (1.75 oz) shrimps, shelled, deveined
50 g (1.75 oz) squid, cleaned, cut into thin rings
2 slices old ginger
1 clove garlic, sliced
1 shallot, sliced
2 tablespoons oil

SEASONING
1 teaspoon salt
½ teaspoon sugar
½ teaspoon light soya sauce

Golden mushrooms, botanically known as Flammulina velutipes, *have long, slender stems and a light creamy colouring. Mild in taste and crisp in texture, golden mushrooms should be cooked for a very short time.*

Button mushrooms, on the other hand, are short and stout with a rubbery texture.

Both are used in this dish to add texture and blend in the rich flavours of the seafood.

Trim off root ends of golden mushrooms. Cut the mushrooms into matchstick lengths. Wash and drain.

Heat 2 tablespoons oil in a wok. When oil is smoking, add ginger, garlic and shallots and fry till fragrant.

Put in carrot, French beans and button mushrooms. Sauté for 3 minutes. Then add prepared seafood and fry for 5 minutes. Lastly, include golden mushrooms.

Season with salt, sugar and light soya sauce and stir fry for 1 minute. Serve immediately.

雙菇豆腐 ●

MUSHROOMS STIR-FRIED WITH BEANCURD

50 g (1.75 oz) dried Chinese mushrooms
½ small carrot, sliced
100 g (3.5 oz) fresh or canned straw mushrooms
300 g (10.5 oz) beancurd (tofu)
30 g (1 oz) sweet peas
1 shallot, sliced
2 slices old ginger
500 ml (2 cups) oil for deep frying beancurd

MARINADE FOR MUSHROOMS
½ teaspoon salt
½ teaspoon sugar
1 teaspoon oil
1 tablespoon cornflour

CORNFLOUR THICKENING
1 tablespoon cornflour
2 tablespoons water

SEASONING
1 teaspoon salt
1 teaspoon sugar
1 teaspoon light soya sauce
½ teaspoon dark soya sauce
1 tablespoon oyster sauce

This is a very simple dish which is rich in protein.

It is an example of the technique where an ingredient is deep fried before it is combined with other ingredients by stir frying.

Trim stems from dried mushrooms. Soak them in 185 ml (¾ cup) water for 30 minutes. Squeeze off excess water and marinate mushrooms. Retain mushroom water for later use. Wash and blanch carrot and straw mushrooms in boiling water for 3 minutes. Drain and discard water.

Cut beancurd into bite-sized pieces. Deep fry in 500 ml (2 cups) hot oil for 2 minutes until light golden brown. Scoop out with a perforated ladle and drain well.

Retain and heat 2 tablespoons of oil in a wok. When hot, put in ginger and shallots and fry till aromatic. Add blanched carrots, straw mushrooms and peas and fry for 1 minute. Remove sweet peas from the wok and leave aside. Pour in mushroom water and bring to a boil. Add in mushrooms and seasoning and continue to simmer for 5 minutes over low heat.

Now include the deep-fried beancurd and cooked sweet peas and continue to simmer for another 2 minutes. Thicken with cornflour mixture and stir for 1 minute. Dish out and serve immediately.

STIR-FRIED SCALLOPS WITH CHICKEN LIVERS

鷄
膶
炒
帶
子
○

400 g (14 oz) fresh scallops
3 chicken livers
100 g (3.5 oz) celery, sliced at a slant into 5 cm (2 inch) lengths
½ small carrot, skinned and sliced
1 clove garlic, sliced
1 shallot, sliced
2 slices old ginger
750 ml (3 cups) oil
1 teaspoon salt

MARINADE FOR CHICKEN LIVERS
½ teaspoon salt
½ teaspoon sugar
½ teaspoon light soya sauce
1 teaspoon Chinese rice wine
1 teaspoon ginger juice
1 tablespoon cornflour
1 tablespoon oil

MARINADE FOR SCALLOPS
¼ teaspoon salt
½ teaspoon sugar
1 teaspoon cornflour
1 teaspoon oil
Dash of pepper

SEASONING
½ teaspoon salt
½ teaspoon sugar
½ tablespoon oyster sauce

The clean taste of fresh scallops and the rich, earthy taste of chicken livers go well with celery.

Rub a teaspoon of salt into the chicken livers and rinse them well to get rid of any odour before marinating.

This dish is good for anaemic persons as both scallops and liver have high iron content.

Clean and rub chicken livers thoroughly with 1 teaspoon of salt. Rinse well. Slice and marinate for 10 minutes. Rinse and drain scallops. Slice into halves. Marinate for 5 minutes. Blanch celery and carrot in boiling water for 1 minute. Drain.

Heat 750 ml (3 cups) oil until hot. Put marinated liver in hot oil for ½ minute to seal juices. Switch off heat and then add in scallops. Remove all ingredients from oil and drain.

Retain 1 tablespoon oil in wok. Reheat till smoky and add in ginger, garlic, and shallots to fry till fragrant.

Add in celery and carrot and fry for 1 minute. Put in the livers, scallops and seasoning. Fry well for 1 minute. Serve immediately.

咕嚕肉

SWEET SOUR PORK

300 g (10.5 oz) pork loin
½ egg, beaten
Cornflour for coating
1 big onion, wedged
1 green big pepper (capsicum), deseeded and wedged
2 canned pineapple rings, wedged
1 red chilli, deseeded and wedged
1 tomato, wedged
2 stalks spring onions, cut into 5 cm (2 inch) lengths
1 shallot, sliced
1 garlic, sliced
1.5 litre (6 cups) oil

MARINADE FOR PORK
1 teaspoon salt
1 teaspoon sugar
1 teaspoon light soya sauce
1 tablespoon cornflour

SAUCE INGREDIENTS
8 tablespoons canned pineapple syrup
1 teaspoon vinegar
2 tablespoons sugar
2 tablespoons tomato ketchup

CORNFLOUR THICKENING
1 tablespoon cornflour
2 tablespoons water

This dish has helped to make Cantonese cooking the most well known among Chinese provincial cuisines, and Sweet Sour Pork has also made the stir frying method famous around the world.

Westerners love this dish and it is to the foreigners who first arrived in Cantonese treay ports during the Qing dynasty that the dish owes its Chinese name. Kuro Yok (咕咾肉) is a deliberate mispronounciation of Kweilo Yok, which means The Meat for the Foreign Devils.

Cantonese chefs created this dish to win the foreigners' tastebuds. They took ingredients familiar to westerners and used Chinese methods to prepare the food. So, slices of pork were dusted with flour and deep fried; vegetables like capsicums, Spanish onions, tomatoes and later, even pineapple, were incorporated. All this was combined in a sauce which used tomato ketchup as a base.

This dish has become a standard in Cantonese restaurants, and I always order Sweet Sour Pork when I patronise a new restaurant. If this dish makes the grade, I know I can have confidence in the rest of their menu.

Wash, dry and cut pork into bite-sized pieces. Marinate for 30 minutes. Dip each piece of pork into the beaten egg, coat evenly with cornflour and press lighly with hand.

Bring 1.5 litre (6 cups) of oil to a boil. Slide in pork and deep-fry for 2 minutes over medium heat until golden brown. Remove and drain. Clean wok.

Heat wok till hot and add in 1 tablespoon oil. Fry shallots and garlic till fragrant. Put in onions, capsicum and chilli. Fry for 1 minute.

Pour in sauce ingredients and bring to a boil. Thicken sauce with cornflour thickening and stir well for 1 minute.

Add deep-fried pork, pineapples, tomatoes and spring onions and mix well for 15 seconds. Dish out and serve hot.

木耳炒猪腰

STIR-FRIED KIDNEYS WITH WOOD FUNGUS

1 pair pig's kidneys
10 g (0.3 oz) wood fungus (*mok yee*), soaked
300 g (10.5 oz) celery, sliced at a slant
½ carrot, skinned and sliced
2 stalks spring onions, sliced into 5 cm (2 inch) lengths
2 slices old ginger, shredded
1 teaspoon Chinese rice wine
2 tablespoons oil

MARINADE FOR KIDNEYS
½ teaspoon salt
½ teaspoon sugar
½ teaspoon light soya sauce
½ teaspoon oil

SEASONING
½ teaspoon salt
½ teaspoon sugar
½ teaspoon light soya sauce

Kidneys stengthen the kidney and cleanse the bladder while celery is added in this dish to combat obesity and improve general health.

Cut each kidney into two lengthwise. Remove the white parts of the kidneys. Score the top in criss-cross fashion and slice the kidneys into 5 cm pieces. Rub kidneys with 1 teaspoon salt. Rinse and drain. Marinate the cleaned kidneys with seasoning for 5 minutes.

Heat 1 tablespoon oil in wok until hot. Add half the shredded ginger and fry until fragrant. Put in sliced carrots and fry for 3 minutes. Then add wood fungus, celery and seasoning and fry for 2 minutes. Dish out and set aside.

Heat 1 tablespoon oil in a wok. When oil is smoking, add remaining ginger and fry until fragrant. Put in marinated kidneys and cook for 2 minutes. Add Chinese rice wine and spring onions.

Finally, add the cooked vegetables and fry for 1 minute, mixing the ingredients well. Serve immediately.

黑椒牛柳○

BLACK PEPPER BEEF IN CLAYPOT

300 g (10.5 oz) fillet steak
1 big onion, wedged
1 big green pepper (capsicum), deseeded and wedged
1 red chilli, deseeded and wedged
1 teaspoon chopped shallots
1 teaspoon chopped garlic
1 teaspoon coarsely ground black pepper
2 slices old ginger, chopped
500 ml (2 cups) oil
1 teaspoon Chinese rice wine

MARINADE
½ teaspoon salt
1 teaspoon sugar
½ teaspoon light soya sauce
½ teaspoon oyster sauce
1 teaspoon cornflour
1 teaspoon oil

SEASONING
½ teaspoon salt
1 teaspoon sugar
½ teaspoon light soya sauce

SAUCE INGREDIENTS
½ teaspoon salt
1 teaspoon sugar
1 teaspoon cornflour
1 teaspoon tomato ketchup
1 teaspoon dark soya sauce
3 teaspoons water

Besides woks, claypots can also be used for stir frying. Use a claypot with a single thick handle for easier handling and take care that you increase heat slowly as immediate high heat may crack the pot.

As porous clay absorbs flavours, serve the dish in the claypot. The aroma and presentation will be fully appreciated by your guests.

This stir-fried dish is a comfort food, warming the stomach and stimulating blood circulation.

Slice beef thinly across the grain. Marinate for 15 minutes.

Heat 500 ml (2 cups) oil in a wok. When hot, deep fry marinated beef for 15 seconds. Ladle out and drain.

Heat a claypot with 2 teaspoons of oil. When the oil is smoking, add shallots, garlic, chilli, black pepper and ginger and fry till fragrant.

Add onion and capsicum, fry for 1 minute, then include seasoning.

Mix sauce ingredients and pour it into claypot and cook for 2 minutes. Then stir in beef and fry for 1 minute. Sprinkle in 1 teaspoon Chinese rice wine just before serving. Serve immediately in the claypot.

RICE FRIED WITH EIGHT TREASURES

300 g (2 cups) raw rice
700 ml (3 cups) water
80 g (3 oz) barbecued pork (char siew), diced
80 g (3 oz) Chinese waxed sausage, diced
80 g (3 oz) shelled shrimps, deveined
10 g (0.3 oz) spring onion, chopped
10 g (0.3 oz) blanched Chinese chives (gau wong), chopped
40 g (1.5 oz) steamed crab meat
3 eggs
80 g (3 oz) iceburg lettuce, shredded
750 ml (3 cups) oil

MARINADE FOR PRAWNS
½ teaspoon salt
½ teaspoon sugar
1 tablespoon egg white
1 teaspoon cornflour
Dash of pepper

SEASONING
1 teaspoon salt
1 teaspoon light soya sauce

Yangchow in Kiangsu province is famed for its cuisine, and it was the chefs of this town who created this attractive and nutritious dish. Also known as Yangchow Fried Rice, the dish is popular and grand enough even for formal banquets.

Any ingredient in season can be used as a 'treasure', but the combination should always be colourful and pleasing to the eye. Make sure that the rice is well fried – with rice grains intact, and not too oily.

Wash raw rice briefly under tap water twice. Drain. Put rice into a saucepan with 750 ml (3 cups) water. Cover saucepan. Bring to a boil over high heat and keep boiling for 5 minutes. Lower heat to very low and leave rice to absorb the water for about 10–15 minutes. Leave cooked rice in the saucepan for half an hour then scoop out and leave to cool on a platter for 1 hour before frying.

Marinate shrimps for 20 minutes. Heat 750 ml (3 cups) oil till very hot and deep fry marinated shrimps for 1 minute. Dish out and drain well. Set aside.

Beat 1 egg to make omelette. Heat a wok with 1 tablespoon oil. When hot, pour in the beaten egg and turn the wok so that a thin omelette is formed. Allow to cook to a golden brown on both sides, then dish out, cool and shred. Set aside for garnishing.

Beat the remaining 2 eggs. Reheat wok and add in 1 tablespoon oil. When hot, put in the 2 beaten eggs and scramble till eggs are crumbly. Add the cooked rice and mix well. Add seasoning.

Keep frying and mixing while adding the barbecued pork, Chinese sausage, shrimps, chives and spring onion. Continue frying for another 3 minutes. Dish out the fried rice onto a serving plate. Garnish with crab meat, shredded omelette and lettuce.

大豆芽菜炒肉鬆 ●

STIR-FRIED SOYA BEANSPROUTS WITH PORK

400 g (14 oz) soya beansprouts (*tai dau ngar choy*)
200 g (7 oz) minced pork
10 g (0.3 oz) coriander, chopped
10 g (0.3 oz) spring onions, chopped
2 slices old ginger, minced
2 shallots, minced
2 tablespoons oil

MARINADE FOR PORK
1 teaspoon salt
1 teaspoon sugar
1 teaspoon light soya sauce
1 tablespoon cornflour
1 teaspoon oil
Dash of pepper

SEASONING
1 teaspoon salt
1 teaspoon sugar
1 teaspoon light soya sauce
½ teaspoon dark soya sauce

CORNFLOUR THICKENING
1 tablespoon cornflour
2 tablespoons water

The colloquial Chinese name for soya beans is tai dau (*literally, big beans*). *So, soya beansprouts are known as* tai dau ngar choy *or big beansprouts.*

Though soya beansprouts are less tender than mung beansprouts, they are more nutritious and more economical. Soya beansprouts should be blanched with water mixed with old ginger before cooking. This is to get rid of its rawness and 'cooling' properties.

When I was a child, I was often told a bedtime story about how the Goddess of Mercy used a needle to pierce a whole sack of soya beans as a trial leading towards enlightenment. Next time you come across soya beansprouts, take a close look at the cotyledons and you will always find two pin pricks on each of them.

Trim off roots of soya beansprouts. Wash and drain sprouts, and then chop coarsely. Marinate pork for 10 minutes.

Heat 1 tablespoon oil in a wok. When hot, add half the ginger and shallots and fry till fragrant.

Put in beansprouts and seasoning and fry for 3 minutes or until dry. Dish out and set aside.

Reheat wok and add 1 tablespoon oil. When the oil is smoking, fry the remaining ginger and shallots till fragrant. Now include the marinated pork and fry a further 5 minutes.

Finally, stir in the soya beansprouts and fry for 1 minute. Add cornflour thickening and stir for 2 minutes. Add in spring onions and coriander, then dish up and serve hot.

生
蠔
煲
○

OYSTERS IN A CLAYPOT

Oysters are universally acknowledged as a superior shellfish. This dish shows how the Chinese eat their oysters.

Oysters are rich in iron and calcium, so this claypot dish is a restorative beneficial to those who are anaemic.

500 g (1 lb) shelled fresh oysters
1 clove garlic, sliced
1 tablespoon fermented black beans, rinsed and mashed
1 red chilli, deseeded and sliced (optional)
1 medium-sized Spanish onion, sliced
50 g (1.75 oz) young ginger roots, sliced
300 g (10.5 oz) spring onions, cut into 5 cm (2 inch) lengths
100 g (3.5 oz) coriander leaves, cut into 5 cm (2 inch) lengths
1 teaspoon salt
2 teaspoons sugar
½ teaspoon light soya sauce
1 tablespoon Chinese rice wine
Dash of pepper
2 tablespoons oil

Rinse and drain oysters.

Heat claypot with 1 tablespoon oil until the oil begins to smoke.

Fry garlic, fermented black beans and chilli for 1 minute until fragrant. Add Spanish onions and ginger roots and fry for 2 minutes.

Include spring onions and coriander leaves. Then, salt, sugar, light soya sauce and remaining oil. Fry well for 1 minute.

Now add the oysters and stir. Cover lid for 1 minute.

Sprinkle in Chinese rice wine and dash of pepper just before serving.

Serve immediately in claypot.

FLAT RICE NOODLES STIR-FRIED WITH BEANSPROUTS

干炒河粉

300 g (10.5 oz) flat rice noodles (*sar hor fun*)
150 g (5.5 oz) beansprouts, roots removed
100 g (3.5 oz) blanched Chinese chives (*gau wong*),
    cut into 5 cm (2 inch) lengths
20 g (0.7 oz) spring onions, shredded finely
1 red chilli, deseeded and sliced
2 slices old ginger
2 shallots, sliced
1 clove garlic, sliced
3 tablespoons oil
1 tablespoon sesame seeds

SEASONING
1 teaspoon salt
1 teaspoon sugar
1 tablespoon dark soya sauce
1 teaspoon sesame oil

Flat rice noodles are made by grinding rice in water, after which the resulting thin batter is spread thinly on a steaming tray and cooked for a very short while. The result is a delicate sheet of rice pasta which is cut into noodles.

To acheive a good smooth texture, the quality of the water used for grinding the rice is important. There is a small town, with a river running through it, on the outskirts of Canton. It is called Sar Hor 沙河, or literally Sandy River. The water of this river is so pure that when used to make steamed rice noodles, it produces the best results. No wonder the Chinese call this type of noodle Sar Hor Fun – Noodles from Sar Hor.

Flat rice noodles are sold stuck together. Separate them into individual noodles by hand.

Pan-fry the sesame seeds in a dry wok (without oil) over low heat until light golden brown. Dish out and cool.

Heat 1 tablespoon oil in a wok. When hot, add ginger, shallots and garlic and fry till fragrant. Include beansprouts and chives and fry for 1 minute. Dish out and put aside.

Reheat wok with the remaining 2 tablespoons of oil and add in the flat rice noodles. Fry for 2 minutes, add in the seasoning and fry for another 1 minute. Now toss in the beansprouts mixture and fry for 30 seconds.

Dish out cooked ingredients onto a serving plate. Garnish with spring onions and chilli. Sprinkle the sesame seeds on top and serve hot.

STIR-FRIED MUSTARD GREENS

500 g (1 lb) mustard greens *(choy sum)*
1 clove garlic, chopped
1 shallot, chopped
2 slices old ginger, shredded
2 tablespoons oil

SEASONING
1 teaspoon salt
1 teaspoon sugar
1 teaspoon light soya sauce
1 tablespoon oyster sauce
½ teaspoon Chinese rice wine

Rinse the mustard greens and discard any whithered leaves. Drain.

Heat a wok till hot. Put in 2 tablespoons oil and when smoky, add in garlic, shallot and ginger. Fry till fragrant.

Include drained vegetable and stir fry briskly for 1 minute over high flame.

Add in seasoning and fry well for 1 more minute. If too dry, add in 2 teaspoons water and stir well. Dish and serve immediately.

Choose young mustard greens which are about the same size for stir frying. They should not be flowering as flowers indicate older plants. Also, their stems should not be fibrous.

This is one of the most basic stir-fried dishes. It is quick to prepare and easily digestible. After cooking, the vegetables should be tender and yet remain crispy and bright green. At the same time, the mustard greens should be coated with a shiny film of oil without being greasy to the taste.

桂
花
翅

SCRAMBLED SHARK'S FIN, CRAB MEAT & EGGS

200 g (7 oz) soaked shark's fins
100 g (3.5 oz) steamed crab meat
6 eggs
100 g (3.5 oz) beansprouts, remove heads and roots
10 g (0.3 oz) Chinese ham, shredded
10 g (0.3 oz) spring onion, shredded finely
10 g (0.3 oz) coriander, shredded finely
1 small head iceburg lettuce
2-3 tablespoons oil

SEASONING
1 teaspoon salt
1 teaspoon sugar
1 teaspoon sesame oil
Dash of pepper

FOR SCALDING SHARK'S FIN
2 slices old ginger
1 stalk spring onion
1 tablespoon Chinese rice wine
1.3 litres (5 cups) water

This impressive southern Chinese dish is often served in Cantonese restaurants as a starter. Rich in nutrients, it is also good for one's complexion.

Use loose shark's fin for this classy dish. Make sure that all cartilage is removed from the steamed crab meat; any shell and cartilage left in will spoil the pleasure in eating this expensive dish.

The secret of stir frying this dish is the control of heat. Decrease the flame from high to low as you stir in the eggs. This is to prevent the scrambled eggs from getting too dry.

Peel the lettuce into individual leaves. Choose the palm-sized ones. Rinse and pat dry thoroughly and set aside.

Bring scalding liquid to a boil. Put in shark's fins and simmer for 15 minutes. Drain shark's fins thoroughly and discard the scalding liquid, ginger and spring onions.

Heat a wok. Add 1 tablespoon oil, and when hot, put in beansprouts and ½ teaspoon salt and fry for 30 seconds. Dish out and set aside.

Break eggs in a big bowl. Add in seasoning and beat well. Add drained shark's fins, steamed crab meat, shredded Chinese ham and the sautéed beansprouts.

Heat a wok till hot. Add in 1 tablespoon of oil and when very hot, pour in the egg mixture and start stirring. Quickly switch heat to low and keep stirring to make scrambled eggs. If more oil is needed, it should be gradually added in during the stirring process.

Keep stirring. The dish is ready when the eggs are fluffy, dry and well scrambled. Dish onto a serving plate and garnish with shredded spring onions and coriander. Serve with the lettuce. Guests serve themselves, putting the scambled ingredients into lettuce leaves.

PORK STIR-FRIED WITH MIXED VEGETABLES

肉絲什菜

This dish is similar to the famous mixed vegetable dish known to westerners as chop suey.

More correctly known as sum choy 什菜 or literally, an assortment of vegetables, it is not a vegetarian dish since pork and garlic are among the ingredients. Here, the pork gives this vegetable dish a sweet, meaty flavour.

150 g (5.5 oz) pork fillet, shredded
150 g (5.5 oz) beansprouts, roots removed
3 Chinese mushrooms, soaked and shredded
150 g (5.5 oz) Chinese cabbage (*pak choy*), shredded
½ small carrot, skinned and shredded
10 g (0.3 oz) wood fungus, soaked and shredded coarsely
80 g (3 oz) mungbean vermicelli (*fun see*), soaked and drained
1 clove garlic, sliced
1 shallot, sliced
2 slices of old ginger, shredded
750 ml (3 cups) oil

MARINADE FOR PORK
1 teaspoon salt
1 teaspoon sugar
½ teaspoon light soya sauce
1 teaspoon cornflour
1 teaspoon oil

SEASONING
1 teaspoon salt
1 teaspoon sugar
1 teaspoon light soya sauce
½ tablespoon oyster sauce

Marinate pork for 10 minutes. Heat the 750 ml (3 cups) of oil in wok and when hot, deep fry the marinated pork for 1 minute to seal in juices. Remove and drain.

Reheat wok with 1 tablespoon oil. When the oil is smoking, add in half the ginger and fry till fragrant. Add in beansprouts and sauté for 1 minute. Dish out and put aside for later use.

Again, reheat the wok with 1 tablespoon oil and when hot, add in the garlic, shallot and remaining ginger. Fry till fragrant and then include the mushrooms and cabbage. Fry well for 3 minutes. Put in the carrot and fungus and fry another 3 minutes.

Add in the seasoning and the drained mungbean vermicelli. Include the precooked pork after 1 minute and mix thoroughly.

Finally, stir in the sautéed beansprouts and mix well.

Serve immediately.

雪耳炒猪干

STIR-FRIED LIVER
WITH SNOW FUNGUS

Liver fortifies the blood and is also good for eyesight.

Sesame oil, extracted from roasted sesame seeds, is added as a flavouring in this dish. This oil, because of its nutty flavour, is not used as a cooking oil, but is mostly used in marinades and as a seasoning just before serving. Remember to use sesame oil sparingly as it is very 'heaty'.

100 g (3.5 oz) pig's liver
1 big green pepper (capsicum), deseeded and cut into big wedges
½ carrot, skinned and sliced
20 g (0.7 oz) snow fungus, soaked and cut into florets
2 slices of old ginger
1 teaspoon salt
½ teaspoon sugar
½ teaspoon light soya sauce
½ teaspoon sesame oil
1 teaspoon Chinese rice wine
1 tablespoon oil
60 ml (¼ cup) water

MARINADE
½ teaspoon salt
½ teaspoon sugar
1 teaspoon oil

Wash and slice liver thickly. Marinate.

Heat 1 tablespoon oil in a wok. When oil is smoking, put in ginger and fry till fragrant. Add sliced carrots and fry for 2 minutes.

Put in snow fungus florets and 60 ml (¼ cup) water. Cover wok and cook for 5 minutes. Include capsicums and fry for 1 minute. Add salt, sugar and light soya sauce.

Lastly, add marinated liver and stir fry quickly for 1 minute (or until liver is cooked). Sprinkle with sesame oil and Chinese rice wine before serving.

杞子炒莧菜

CHINESE SPINACH WITH SCALLOPS & MEDLAR SEEDS

This is a good dish for children.

Chinese spinach, being high in iron and fibre, is good roughage while medlar seeds are good for the eyes.

500 g (1 lb) Chinese spinach (*yen choy*)
30 g (1 oz) dried scallops
50 g (1.75 oz) medlar seeds, rinsed
4 slices old ginger
1 clove garlic, skinned and crushed
1 teaspoon oil
375 ml (1½ cups) warm water

SEASONING
1 teaspoon salt
2 teaspoons oil
½ teaspoon oyster sauce
1 teaspoon sugar

CORNFLOUR THICKENING
1 teaspoon cornflour
2 teaspoons water
½ teaspoon dark soya sauce

Wash and soak scallops in 375 ml (1½ cups) of warm water for 1 hour. Drain but retain water.

Clean and cut Chinese spinach into 10-cm (4-inch) lengths. Rinse and drain.

Heat 1 teaspoon oil in a wok. When oil is smoking, fry ginger and garlic till fragrant. Now include vegetables and seasoning and fry for 5 minutes. Drain well. Arrange Chinese spinach on serving plate.

Put scallops and medlar seeds into the scallop water and boil for 10 minutes over low flame. Add cornflour thickening. Stir well and cook for 2 minutes. Pour this scallop gravy over cooked vegetables and serve hot.

絲瓜炒肉絲 ●

FRIED PORK WITH ANGLED LUFFA

150 g (5.5 oz) lean pork
1 angled luffa (*si kwa*), about 300g (10.5 oz)
10 g (0.3 oz) dried wood fungus (*mok yee*)
1 Spanish onion, wedged
½ small carrot, skinned and sliced
1 clove garlic, sliced
4 slices old ginger
750 ml (3 cups) oil

MARINADE FOR PORK
½ teaspoon salt
½ teaspoon sugar
½ teaspoon light soya sauce
1 teaspoon oyster sauce
1 teaspoon oil

SEASONING
1 teaspoon salt
1 teaspoon sugar
1 teaspoon light soya sauce
½ teaspoon sesame oil, to add before serving
Dash of pepper, to add before serving

This is a 'cooling' dish which is good for alleviating 'heatiness' from the body.

If your body composition is 'cooling' and you love angled luffa, use a few more drops of sesame oil to 'neutralise' the dish.

Slice the pork across the grain thinly. Marinate for 15 minutes. Heat 750 ml (3 cups) of oil in a wok. When hot, deep-fry the sliced pork for 1 minute to seal in the juices. Dish out and drain well.

Wash the wood fungus and soak them in water for 30 minutes. Trim off stems and tear the fungus into pieces. Drain and discard water.

Skin and slice angled luffa into 5-cm (2-inch) slices. Wash and drain. Heat 1 tablespoon of oil in wok until smoky, then add 2 pieces old ginger and fry till fragrant. Add angled luffa and fry for 2 minutes. Dish out and put aside.

Reheat wok with 1 tablespoon oil until smoky. Add garlic, Spanish onions and the remaining ginger and fry till fragrant. Include wood fungus and carrot and fry for 2 minutes. Then put in sautéed angled luffa and seasoning. Mix well.

Finally, include the pork and stir fry ingredients thoroughly for 1 minute. Dish onto serving plate. Sprinkle with sesame oil and pepper just before serving.

豆
腐
炒
鷄
膶
☯

SOFT SOYABEAN CAKES WITH CHICKEN LIVER

300 g (10.5 oz) soft soya bean cake
2 chicken livers, chopped
200 g (7 oz) packet diced mixed vegetables
1 slice of old ginger
½ teaspoon oil

MARINADE
1 teaspoon salt
1 teaspoon light soya sauce
½ teaspoon oyster sauce
1 teaspoon sugar
1 teaspoon cornflour

You will be surprised how a little chicken liver added to a bland ingredient like soft soyabean cake can make a delicious dish.

For the best results, use soft Japanese bean cakes available in supermarkets. This dish is easily digestible, nutritious and therefore most suitable for the young and the old.

Drain bean cakes. Marinate chicken liver with seasoning for 10 minutes. Wash and drain vegetables.

Heat ½ teaspoon oil in a wok. When oil is smoking, put in ginger and fry till fragrant. Add mixed vegetables and fry for 2 minutes.

Now include marinated chicken livers and fry for 2 minutes. Lastly, put in the soft soya bean cakes and mix gently with fried ingredients so that the bean cakes do not break up.

Leave to simmer for 3 minutes. Check seasoning before serving.

豆
角
鬆

◐

STIR-FRIED DICED LONG BEANS & BARBECUE PORK

200 g (7 oz) long beans, diced
100 g (3.5 oz) barbecued pork (*char siew*)
20 g (0.7 oz) Chinese mushrooms
50 g (1.75 oz) fish cake
50 g (1.75 oz) shrimps, shelled, chopped and marinated
2 slices of old ginger
1 shallot, sliced
1 garlic, sliced
1 small head iceburg lettuce
2 teaspoons oil

SEASONING
1 teaspoon salt
1 teaspoon sugar
1 teaspoon light soya sauce
1 teaspoon oyster sauce

MARINADE FOR SHRIMPS
½ teaspoon salt
½ teaspoon sugar
¼ teaspoon light soya sauce

A Chinese saying goes: Study the presentation of a dish to disclose the character of the cook.

This is true, especially for this dish, since every ingredient used here should be cut into equally fine dices. Properly prepared, this dish will no doubt say that the cook is meticulous and takes great care in his technique.

Long beans, favoured by mothers for their children because of its 'neutral' quality, is enhanced by the other ingredients. For a different taste, you may also include diced Chinese waxed sausages to this dish.

Wash and soak mushroom in water. Squeeze off excess water and dice mushrooms. Wash and dice fish cake. Dice barbecued pork. Marinate prawns. Peel lettuce leaves, cut into palm-sized cups and rinse and drain.

Fry mushrooms without oil for 5 minutes. Put aside.

Heat 1 teaspoon of oil in a wok. When the oil is smoking, put in ginger, shallots and garlic. Fry till fragrant.

Include diced long beans, fry for 2 minutes then add salt, sugar and soya sauce. Fry for another 3 minutes. Dish out and set aside.

Heat the wok again with 1 teaspoon oil. When hot, add marinated shrimps. Fry for 1 minute, then add fish cake and barbecued pork. Fry for 1 minute, lower heat and cover wok for 1 more minute before frying again for a further 3 minutes.

Now add mushrooms and long beans. Mix well. Finally, pour in oyster sauce and fry for 2 minutes. Serve hot with lettuce.

苦
瓜
炒
鷄
球
●

FRIED CHICKEN WITH BITTERGOURD

1 bittergourd (about 500 g, 1 lb)
2 chicken thighs
1 red chilli (optional)
1 clove garlic, chopped
2 slices old ginger, chopped
1 tablespoon fermented black beans (*dao si*)
2 tablespoons oil

MARINADE FOR BITTERGOURD

1 teaspoon salt
1 teaspoon sugar

MARINADE FOR CHICKEN

1 teaspoon salt
1 teaspoon sugar
1 teaspoon light soya sauce
1 teaspoon Chinese rice wine
1 tablespoon cornflour
1 tablespoon oil

SEASONING

½ teaspoon salt
1 teaspoon sugar
½ teaspoon light soya sauce

If you want a less bitter bittergourd, choose a just ripened one which has light green skin and is just firm to the touch. However, avoid soft, yellowy gourds. These are over-ripe and are not suitable for stir frying.

Cut bittergourd into halves, lengthwise. Remove seeds and pith. Slice thickly at a slant. Marinate with seasoning for 30 minutes. Rinse with hot water. Squeeze off excess water.

Clean and wash chicken thighs. Debone and cut into thick slices (2 x 5 cm) across the grain. Marinate for 15 minutes.

Deseed and slice red chilli (optional). Rinse and chop fermented black beans.

Heat a claypot with 2 tablespoons oil until smoky. Stir in the garlic, ginger and fermented black beans and fry till fragrant.

Add marinated chicken thighs and fry for 1 minute.

Add bittergourd and seasoning. Fry for a minute then add chilli if preferred. Cover claypot and leave to cook for another 2 minutes.

Serve food sizzling hot in claypot for an authentic effect.

FRIED MUSHROOMS WITH BEANSPROUTS

銀芽冬菇絲 ●

This dish is also known as Vegetarian Eel, with the sliced mushrooms being a substitute for the fish.

The dish benefits the 'yin' essence and improves the complexion.

10 dried Chinese mushrooms
150 g (5.5 oz) beansprouts, tops and roots removed
1 slice old ginger, chopped finely
700 ml (3 cups) oil
Dash of pepper
375 ml (1½ cups) warm water

MARINADE FOR MUSHROOMS
1 teaspoon salt
1 teaspoon sugar
½ teaspoon light soya sauce
½ teaspoon dark soya sauce
1 tablespoon cornflour
1 tablespoon oil

SEASONING
½ teaspoon salt
1 teaspoon sugar

CORNFLOUR THICKENING
1 tablespoon cornflour
2 tablespoons water

Rinse and drain beansprouts. Trim stems from mushrooms. Wash mushrooms and soak them in 375 ml (1½ cups) warm water for 30 minutes. Drain and retain 185 ml (¾ cup) mushroom water. Squeeze off excess water from mushrooms and slice thickly. Marinate for 15 minutes.

Heat 500 ml (2 cups) oil in a wok. When hot, deep fry the marinated mushrooms for 2 minutes to seal juices. Dish out and drain well.

Pour away all but 1 tablespoon oil from the wok. Put in ginger and fry till fragrant. Add beansprouts and fry for 30 seconds until half cooked. Dish out and put aside.

Pour the 175 ml (¾ cup) mushroom water into the wok. Bring to a boil, add in seasoning and stir for 1 minute.

Thicken sauce with cornflour thickening and stir for 1 minute. Add mushrooms and leave to simmer for 2 minutes. When the sauce is very thick, add the beansprouts and mix well. Dish out and season with pepper just before serving.

STIR-FRIED GOLDEN MUSHROOM WITH SCALLOPS

金菇炒瑤柱

●

500 g (1 lb) fresh golden mushrooms
20 g (0.7 oz) dried scallops
1 carrot about 400 g (14 oz), skinned and shredded
100 g (3.5 oz) beansprouts, roots removed
20 g (0.7 oz) spring onions, finely shredded
3 slices old ginger
3 tablespoons oil
125 ml (½ cup) warm water

SAUCE
½ teaspoon salt
1 teaspoon sugar
1 teaspoon ginger juice
Dash of pepper

CORNFLOUR THICKENING
1 tablespoon cornflour
2 tablespoons water

Golden mushrooms tend to be a little bland so dried scallops, an ingredient with a lingering aftertaste, is added to finish the dish.

This colourful and delicious dish is good for replenishing the 'yin' essence and is popular during the hot season.

Rinse and soak dried scallops in 125 ml (½ cup) warm water for 1 hour. Tear scallops into tiny strips. Retain scallop water for sauce.

Trim off the ends of golden mushrooms. Cut the mushrooms into 5 cm lengths. Rinse and drain.

Wash and drain carrot. Wash and drain beansprouts.

Heat 1 tablespoon oil in a wok. When hot, add in half of the ginger and half of the spring onions and fry till fragrant. Then add in the beansprouts and fry for 1 minute. Dish out and put aside. Repeat for shredded carrots.

Reheat wok with 1 tablespoon oil until hot. Fry dried scallop strips for 1 minute, then add in sauce ingredients and the scallop water. Bring to a boil and keep boiling for 2 minutes.

Thicken this sauce with the cornflour thickening. Keep stirring for 2 minutes.

Add golden mushrooms and fry for 1 minute. Finally, include the shredded carrots and beansprouts. Mix well and dish up.

Serve immediately.

STIR-FRIED CHICKEN WITH YOUNG GINGER & PINEAPPLE

子蘿炒鷄
○

If you were to ask me if there is a rival to Sweet Sour Pork, I'd say, try this dish and see for yourself.

I enjoy the combination of crisp young ginger and the juicy pineapple bits. Besides, ginger alleviates 'wind' from the body and stimulates the appetite.

2 chicken thighs
100 g (3.5 oz) young ginger roots, skinned and wedged
4 pieces canned pineapple rings, wedged
1 big green pepper (capsicum), deseeded and wedged
1 red chilli, deseeded and wedged
1 teaspoon chopped garlic
1 teaspoon chopped shallots
1 tablespoon oil

MARINADE FOR CHICKEN
½ teaspoon salt
½ teaspoon sugar
½ teaspoon light soya sauce
½ tablespoon cornflour
1 tablespoon oil

PICKLING FOR GINGER ROOTS
½ teaspoon salt
½ teaspoon sugar
1 tablespoon oil

SAUCE INGREDIENTS, MIXED TOGETHER
½ teaspoon salt
½ teaspoon sugar
1 tablespoon cornflour
4 tablespoons canned pineapple syrup

Pickle ginger roots for 1 hour. Drain.

Wash and debone chicken thighs. Cut into bite-sized pieces. Marinate for 10 minutes.

Heat 1 tablespoon oil in a wok. When oil is smoking, sauté garlic and shallots until fragrant. Add in pickled ginger roots.

Now include marinated chicken and stir fry for 5 minutes.

Add capsicum, chilli and pineapples and fry for another 3 minutes. Add pre-mixed sauce ingredients and stir briskly for 2 minutes. Serve immediately.

蘋
果
炒
鷄
腎

STIR-FRIED CHICKEN GIZZARDS WITH APPLES

6 chicken gizzards
50 g (1.75 oz) raw cashew nuts
2 small red apples
1 big green pepper (capsicum), deseeded and diced coarsely
1 teaspoon chopped shallots
500 ml (2 cups) oil
1 teaspoon salt

MARINADE FOR GIZZARDS
½ teaspoon salt
1 teaspoon sugar
½ teaspoon light soya sauce
½ tablespoon cornflour
1 teaspoon ginger juice
1 teaspoon Chinese rice wine

SALT WATER
750 ml (3 cups) water
1 teaspoon salt

SEASONING
½ teaspoon salt
½ teaspoon sugar
½ teaspoon sesame oil
½ tablespoon oyster sauce
1 tablespoon oil
2 tablespoons water

Originally from South America, cashew nuts were introduced to China during the Qing dynasty. Attempts to cultivate the tree in China proved unsuccessful although the plant flourishes in Southeast Asia.

Cashew nuts are rich in oil and together with chicken gizzards, make a dish which is recommended to those who want a glowing complexion.

Boil cashew nuts in half the salt water for 5 minutes. Drain and wipe dry. Heat 500 ml (2 cups) of oil in a wok. Deep fry nuts in oil until golden brown. Drain and cool. Retain 1 tablespoon of oil in the wok.

Core apples and dice coarsely. Soak in the remaning salt water for 5 minutes. Drain before cooking.

Clean and rub chicken gizzards thoroughly with 1 teaspoon salt. Rinse well. Score the gizzards criss-cross fashion and dice. Marinate for 10 minutes.

Heat the oil in a wok. When it is smoking, sauté shallots, capsicum and apples for 1 minute. Add seasoning.

Add marinated gizzards and fry well for 5 minutes. Then include nuts and mix well. Serve immediately.

STIR-FRIED KALE WITH FISH FILLET

芥蘭炒魚片 ◐

500 g (1 lb) kale (kai lan)
300 g (10.5 oz) white fish fillet
½ small carrot, skinned and sliced
4 button mushrooms, sliced
2 slices old ginger, shredded
1 clove garlic, chopped
1 shallot, chopped
2 tablespoons oil
1 teaspoon Chinese rice wine

BLANCHING SOLUTION
1.5 litres (6 cups) water
1 teaspoon salt
1 teaspoon oil

MARINADE FOR FISH
½ teaspoon salt
½ teaspoon sugar
½ teaspoon light soya sauce
½ teaspoon cornflour
1 teaspoon oil

SEASONING
1 teaspoon salt
1 teaspoon sugar
1 teaspoon light soya sauce
1 tablespoon oyster sauce

The thick stems of kale should be prepared for stir frying by peeling off the fibrous layer to reveal their sweet and succulent centres. And the leaves of kale are thick and crunchy, so the vegetable requires a longer cooking time than other leafy vegetables.

White fish fillet, on the other hand, requires very short cooking time, and they should be well cooked and still remain in slices after stir frying.

This use of hard and tender ingredients requires care and skill during the stir frying process to produced a well cooked dish. Chinese cooks often add a few drops of Chinese rice wine to enhance the taste of both vegetable and fish.

Gut and clean the fish. Pat dry with kitchen towels. Cut into thin slices across the grain. Marinate for 5 minutes.

Slice off fibrous parts of the kale stem. Cut kale slantwise in thick slices. Wash and drain.

Bring 1.5 litres (6 cups) water to a boil. Add 1 teaspoon each of salt and oil. Blanch the kale, carrot and mushrooms in this solution for 2 minutes. Drain and discard liquid.

Heat a wok till hot. Add 2 tablespoons oil and when smoky, put in ginger, garlic and shallots and fry till fragrant. Add the blanched ingredients and fry for 1 minute over high heat. Add seasoning.

Include marinated fish and fry well for 1 minute over high heat. Fry briskly for another 30 seconds and then sprinkle in 1 teaspoon of Chinese rice wine just before dishing out. Serve hot.

BITTERGOURD & SHRIMP OMELETTE

蝦仁炒苦瓜 ☯

1 bittergourd (approx 300 g, 10.5 oz)
50 g (2 oz) shrimps, shelled
3 eggs, beaten
2 slices old ginger
2 tablespoons oil

MARINADE FOR BITTER GOURD
1 teaspoon salt
2 teaspoons sugar

MARINADE FOR SHRIMPS
½ teaspoon salt
½ teaspoon sugar
½ tablespoon oil

SEASONING
½ teaspoon salt
1 teaspoon sugar
½ teaspoon light sauce

As most people do not like the sharp bitterness of this gourd, let me share a little secret of how you can get rid of the bitterness.

All you have to do is to marinate the gourds with a mixture of salt and sugar for 30 minutes; rinse with hot water and dry well before cooking. The proportion of salt and sugar is shown in the recipe.

Bittergourds are best eaten during the hot season.

Wash and cut bittergourd into half lengthwise. Remove pith and seeds. Slice thinly at a slant. Marinate for ½ hour, then scald in hot water for 1 minute. Drain well and set aside. Marinate shrimp for 5 minutes.

Heat 1 tablespoon of oil in a wok. When the oil is smoking, put in ginger and fry till fragrant.

Add bittergourd. Fry for 2 minutes, then add seasoning. Fry for another 3 minutes.

Now include shrimps and fry for 2 minutes.

Add 1 tablespoon of oil and when hot, pour in beaten eggs. Stir fry for 2 minutes and when omelette is set, dish out and serve hot.

銀芽炒牛柳 ◑

SHREDDED BEEF WITH BEANSPROUTS

200 g (7 oz) beef fillet
200 g (7 oz) beansprouts, roots removed
1 big green pepper (capsicum), deseeded and sliced thinly
1 Spanish onion, sliced
1 red chilli, deseeded and chopped roughly
1 clove garlic, chopped
2 slices old ginger
750 ml (3 cups) oil
1 teaspoon Chinese rice wine

MARINADE FOR BEEF
½ teaspoon salt
½ teaspoon sugar
½ teaspoon light soya sauce
½ teaspoon oyster sauce
1 tablespoon cornflour
1 tablespoon oil
Dash of pepper

SEASONING
½ teaspoon salt
1 teaspoon sugar

This light and colourful dish gives strength since both beef and bean-sprouts are high in protein.

It is one of my favourites which I serve all the year round.

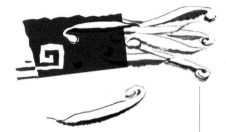

Slice beef thinly (½ cm, ¼ inch) across the grain. Marinate for 30 minutes.

Heat a wok and pour in 750 ml (3 cups) oil. When oil is hot, deep-fry marinated beef for 15 seconds to seal the juices. Drain the beef well.

Pour away all but 2 tablespoons of the oil. Reheat till smoky, then add garlic and ginger and fry till fragrant. Include the onions and capsicum and fry for 2 minutes. Put in beansprouts and seasoning and stir briskly for 1 more minute.

Finally, put in the beef and chilli. Fry for 30 seconds then sprinkle in 1 teaspoon of Chinese rice wine. Dish out and serve immediately.

STIR-FRIED SOYABEAN CAKE WITH CHINESE CHIVE BUDS

韭菜花炒豆干 ●

4 Chinese mushrooms, soaked and sliced thinly
1 piece soyabean cake (*dao korn*), sliced thickly
100 g (3.5 oz) beansprouts, roots removed
50 g (1.75 oz) lean pork, sliced and seasoned lightly
100 g (3.5 oz) Chinese chive buds (*gau choy fa*), cut into 5 cm (2 in) lengths
3 tablespoons oil
1 slice old ginger

SEASONING
1 teaspoon salt
1 teaspoon sugar
½ teaspoon light soya sauce

Chinese chive buds, which have a mild onion taste, are the flowering stalks of Chinese chives. Don't discard the buds; they are edible and the item is pricey because of them.

Choose the stalks with smaller buds as this indicates that the stalks are younger and, therefore, more tender.

Fry mushrooms without oil for 3 minutes. Put aside.

Heat 1 tablespoon of oil in a wok. When hot, add sliced soyabean cake and fry for 3 minutes. Dish out and set aside.

Heat the wok again with 1 tablespoon oil. When oil is smoking, add ginger and fry till fragrant. Include Chinese chive buds and fry for 2 minutes, then put in beansprouts. Add seasoning and fry for 2 minutes. Dish out and set aside.

Heat wok once again with 1 tablespoon oil. When hot, put in seasoned lean pork and fry for 5 minutes. Add mushrooms and soyabean cake. Mix well.

Lastly, add in stir-fried vegetables and toss well. Serve immediately.

皮蛋炒牛肉 ○ STIR-FRIED BEEF WITH CENTURY EGG

2 century eggs
200 g (7 oz) beef fillet
100 g (3.5 oz) preserved young ginger roots (*chee keong*)
1 teaspoon sesame seeds
750 ml (3 cups) oil

MARINADE FOR BEEF
1 teaspoon salt
1 teaspoon sugar
1 teaspoon oyster sauce
1 tablespoon cornflour
1 tablespoon oil

SEASONING
1 teaspoon Chinese rice wine
1 teaspoon sugar

Shell century eggs. Rinse, dry and slice each egg into six wedges.

Drain liquid from preserved young ginger roots. Squeeze off excess liquid from ginger roots and set the ginger roots aside.

Fry the sesame seeds in a wok without oil over low heat until they turn light golden brown. Cool.

Cut beef into thin slices across the grain. Marinate for 30 minutes.

Heat 750 ml (3 cups) oil in wok. Slide in the marinated beef and deep fry for 15 seconds to seal in juices. Dish out and drain.

Pour away all but 1 tablespoon oil from the wok. Reheat wok and when smoky, add in the beef, century eggs and ginger roots. Stir fry for 30 seconds, add seasoning and continue frying for another 30 seconds.

Dish out and sprinkle with browned sesame seeds just before serving.

Century eggs are pungent and somewhat an acquired taste. Yet, I have loved eating century eggs since my childhood.

My gongfu master told me that I should eat plenty of century eggs if I had bruises from his lessons. This is because the Chinese believe that century eggs can purify the blood.

Do not let the implied age of the eggs baffle you. Actually, the eggs are preserved for closer to a hundred days than a hundred years.

Century eggs are always served with young ginger roots and this dish is no exception.

STEAMING

Steaming: valued for its simplicity and ability to retain natural flavours.

Steaming is one of the most popular cooking methods used in the Chinese kitchen. It is cooking food by steam with the food being placed above the waterline in a vessel of boiling water.

This arrangement is reflected in the Chinese character for 'steaming' – 蒸. The character has two main parts, 烝 which means to hold up or support, and 灬 which is the ideogram for heat from fire. These two components are separated by a line representing a container or tray, and together they summarise perfectly this method of cooking.

Steaming is valued for its simplicity and its ability to retain the natural flavours of each ingredient. It is also a healthy way of cooking since very little oil is used. Steamed food is considered non-heaty (not possessing the 'yang' element), and therefore favoured by the Chinese. The process is practical too. It is convenient, tidy and saves time. Left-overs can be re-steamed without losing flavour or food value. Apart from these advantages, a wide variety of food can be cooked by steaming. These include seafood, poultry, beancurd and pork.

Several points should be observed when steaming food. Always use fresh ingredients so that their subtle flavours can be savoured. For the same reason, serve steamed food immediately after the dish is ready. Ingredients should be seasoned before steaming, but the amount of seasoning should be carefully controlled so that the original tastes of the foods are not masked. To enhance flavour and to retain the natural juices of the food, ingredients may be placed on, or wrapped in, aromatic leaves such as lotus leaves or banana leaves.

There are two types of steaming: clear steaming 清蒸 and dry steaming 干蒸. Ingredients to be cooked by clear steaming are prepared by seasoning them with light soya sauce, Chinese rice wine, oil or other seasonings. The result is a dish with a delicious, light gravy that is full of natural goodness. A classic example is Fish Steamed on Lotus Leaf (see page 107). For dry steaming, the seasoned food is wrapped in dough or skins. No sauces are used and the food values and flavour of the ingredients are locked inside the wrapping. Dim sums items such as siew mai and char siew buns are good examples.

For basic steaming, you will need a wok with a cover, an enamel or porcelain plate and a stainless steel tripod. Place the tripod in the wok and fill the wok until the water-level is 2.5 cm (1 inch) below the platform of the tripod. Cover the wok and bring the water to a boil over high heat.

In every case, the water must be boiling before the prepared food is placed in the steamer. Place the prepared plate of food on the tripod and cover the wok. Set the heat to the appropriate level according to the recipe and cook for the required time. To increase the temperature in the wok, put damp towels around the edge of the lid to prevent steam from escaping.

As a rule, the steamer should not be opened when the food being cooked (e.g. fish) need only be steamed for a short time. In this case, there must be enough water boiling steadily to produce steam during the whole cooking period. However, with foods that require a longer cooking time (e.g. whole chicken), the water-level must be checked occasionally and maintained by adding boiling water.

Although the steaming process is simple, different foods and recipes call for variations to the technique. Some of them require special kitchenware which can be found in Chinese hardware shops.

Perforated plate steaming involves the use of a perforated metal plate. The process is identical to the basic steaming method except that the perforated plate is placed on the tripod to hold several small plates or bowls of the same food which can then be steamed at one time. Steamed Egg Custard (pg 99) is a good example.

Steaming with large bamboo steamers allow many items of the same food to be cooked together. These steamers have slatted bottoms which allow steam to rise through them, and two or three layers of steamers are usually used at a time. Each bamboo steamer is lined with either fragrant leaves or perforated plates and the prepared food is placed on them. The steamers are stacked and the top layer covered with the lid. The whole arrangement is then placed over boiling water and steamed. The water-level in the wok should be 5 cm (2 inches) from the bottom steamer. Many dim sum dishes are cooked by this method.

Distil Steaming uses a Yunnan steam pot. Originating from China's Yunnan province, this covered earthern tureen has a spout on its base which allows steam to enter the pot. Prepared food is put in the pot around the spout and the steam which enters the pot not only cooks the food but is also distilled to add pure water to the ingredients. Traditionally, the Yunnan steam pot was placed over a tightly-fitting pot of boiling water wrapped with damp cloth to prevent the steam from escaping. However, the pot can also be placed on a tripod in a large saucepan of water. Leave about 5 cm (2 inches) clearance between the base of the Yunnan pot and the boiling water.

KITCHENWARE

Wok with lid
Stainless steel tripod
Round metal perforated plate
Bamboo steamers with lid
Porcelain or enamel plate
Yunnan steam pot

INGREDIENTS SUITABLE FOR STEAMING

SEAFOOD	FRAGRANT LEAVES	MISCELLANEOUS	MEAT
Fish	Lotus leaves	Egg	Sliced or minced pork
Shrimp	Pandanus leaves	Beancurd	Chicken
Squid	Banana leaves		
Crab			

TEMPERATURE AND COOKING TIMES

1.5 kg (3.3 lb) *Poultry*, 45 minutes at medium heat
Sliced Pork (regardless of weight), 15 minutes at medium heat
Fish (200 g or 7 oz), 5 minutes at high heat
Unshelled Shrimps, 5 minutes at high heat
Squids, 5 minutes at high heat
Whole Crabs, 15 minutes at high heat
Egg custards, 15 minutes at low heat
Dim Sums, on the average 10 minutes at high heat
Buns, 10 to 15 minutes at high heat
Beancurds, 10 minutes at high heat

百花豆腐 ◑

STEAMED STUFFED BEANCURD

4 squares soft beancurd
200 g (7 oz) prawns
200 g (7 oz) fillet of white fish
4 water chestnuts
10 g (0.3 oz) spring onion
10 g (0.3 oz) coriander leaves
300 g (10.5 oz) mustard green (choy sum)

PRAWN & FISH PASTE SEASONING
1 teaspoon salt
1 teaspoon sugar
Dash of pepper

CORNFLOUR MIXTURE
1 teaspoon cornflour
1 teaspoon water

SAUCE
1 teaspoon salt
1 teaspoon sugar
2 teaspoons light soya sauce
1 teaspoon dark soya sauce
2 tablespoons oil

FOR BLANCHING MUSTARD GREEN
1.3 litres (5 cups) boiling water
1 teaspoon salt
1 tablespoon oil

The success of this recipe depends on one's skill in making a springy prawn and fish paste as well as delicately hollowing out the beancurd for the stuffing.

I used to get scolded by my father because I scooped out so much of the beancurd that the beancurd shell would burst when it was filled.

This nutritious dish is good for all the family as it is well-balanced with protein and iron.

Shell and devein prawns. Rinse and pat thoroughly dry. Use the flat of a cleaver to flatten the prawns, then mince to a paste. Mince the fish fillet into a paste.

Mix both prawn paste and fish paste together. Add seasoning. Take handfuls of the mixture and slap on the side of a large bowl until a springy and slightly firm texture is obtained.

Wash and skin water chestnuts. Dice finely. Add to prawn and fish paste. Also include the chopped spring onion and coriander leaves.

Rinse beancurd and pat dry thoroughly. Cut each beancurd diagonally and scoop out some beancurd on the cut side to make a hollow. Fill the hollow with the mixture and seal the surface with some cornflour mixture. Repeat with the remaining beancurd. Place stuffed beancurd on a steaming dish, mix the sauce well and pour it over the stuffed beancurd. Steam for 10 minutes over high flame.

While the beancurd is being cooked, wash and blanch the mustard greens in the blanching solution for 2 minutes. Drain the vegetables well.

Serve the steamed beancurd with mustard greens. Garnish with shredded spring onions and coriander leaves.

STEAMED HONEY PEARS

蜜汁雪梨 ●

4 Chinese pears with stalks (*shuet lei*)
100 g (3.5 oz) sweet and bitter almond mixture (see page 213)
4 tablespoons honey
625 ml (2½ cups) water

SALT SOLUTION FOR PEARS
625 ml (2½ cups) water
1 teaspoon salt

Two of the most popular varieties of Chinese pear are Sandy Pear 沙梨 and Snow Pear 雪梨. As the names imply, the latter has a more velvety texture, yet it is still crisp to the bite.

The older folk of my family fancy this dish. They believe that this refreshing snack and dessert is good for soothing the throat and the lungs.

Peel pears and retain stalks. Soak pears in salt water for 3 minutes. Drain.

Bring 625 ml (2½ cups) water to a boil. Add in almond mixture and leave to boil for 10 minutes over low flame. Add honey and stir for a minute. Switch off heat.

Pour this solution, together with the almond mixture, into a big bowl and put in all the pears. Steam for 1 hour or until pears are soft.

To serve, put the steamed pears into individual dessert bowls and spoon about 6 tablespoons of the almond and honey sauce over each pear. Serve hot or chilled.

CHICKEN & SNOW FUNGUS IN YUNNAN POT

雪耳汽鍋雞 ◐

½ chicken, about 750g (1.6 lb)
10 g (0.3 oz) snow fungus
50 g (1.75 oz) Yunnan ham
10 g (0.3 oz) sweet and bitter almond mixture (see page 213)
2.5 litres (10 cups) hot water
1 teaspoon salt, or to taste

Using a Yunnan pot makes this soup clear and distinctive. Crunchy and nutritious snow fungus is added to give texture to this distilled broth to which taste is enhanced by the addition of superior quality Yunnan ham.

Including a small amount of sweet and bitter almond mixture helps to give the soup the reputation of being able to soothe the lungs.

Clean and wash chicken. Cut chicken into big pieces. Scald in 1 litre (4 cups) hot water for 3 minutes. Drain and rinse. Soak snow fungus in water for 1 hour. Remove stems and tear fungus into florets. Rinse and drain. Rinse almonds briefly. Scald Yunnan ham in 240 ml (1 cup) hot water for 1 minute to remove excess fat. Cut into small cubes.

Put all ingredients and 1.3 litres (5 cups) hot water in a Yunnan pot. Cover and place pot on a tripod in a big wok. The water level should be 5 cm (2 inches) away from the base of the pot. Steam over medium heat for 1½ hours.

Season with salt, if required, before serving. Serve hot in Yunnan pot.

蝦子豆腐 ☯

STEAMED BEANCURD WITH SHRIMP ROE

8 small pieces of soft beancurd
200 g (7 oz) prawns
10 g (0.3 oz) shrimp roe
10 g (0.3 oz) spring onions, shredded finely
10 g (0.3 oz) coriander leaves, shredded finely
1 red chilli, deseeded and sliced finely

SAUCE
½ teaspoon salt
1 tablespoon oyster sauce
1 teaspoon sugar
1 teaspoon oil
½ teaspoon dark soya sauce
½ teaspoon light soya sauce
250 ml (1 cup) water

CORNFLOUR THICKENING
1 tablespoon cornflour
2 tablespoons water

SEASONING
1 teaspoon salt
1 teaspoon oil

MARINADE FOR PRAWNS
½ teaspoon salt
1 teaspoon sugar
1 teaspoon oil

The Chinese use sun-dried shrimp roe to make sauces, and cooks sprinkle them on bland ingredients as a flavouring. Shrimp roe is available from shops selling Chinese delicacies.

Saltwater prawns produce roe that is scarlet and has a strong fishy taste. Freshwater prawns, on the other hand, have smaller, purplish-red eggs. The freshwater roe is less fishy, yet more flavourful, and also more expensive.

Because I love the taste of the shrimp roe, I used to sprinkle more than enough roe on this nutritious and appetising dish at the risk of upsetting the 'yin' and 'yang' balance of the beancurd and roe.

Shell and devein prawns. Rinse and drain. Marinate for 5 minutes.

Wash and drain beancurd thoroughly. Place beancurd onto steaming plate and sprinkle the seasoning over the beancurd. Arrange the marinated prawns over the beancurd and steam for 10 minutes over high heat.

In the meantime, put all the seasoning for the sauce in a saucepan and bring it to a boil for 5 minutes. Add in cornflour thickening and stir well for 2 minutes.

When the beancurd is ready, remove the plate from the steamer and drain off the steamed liquid.

Pour the heated sauce over the steamed beancurd and prawns. Sprinkle the shrimp roe on top of beancurd and garnish with shredded spring onion, coriander leaves and red chilli before serving.

兒
孫
滿
堂

ALL IN THE FAMILY

120 g (4.2 oz) fried fish maws (*zao yu tou*)
300 g (10.5 oz) prawns
10 g (0.3 oz) shrimp roe
300 g (10.5 oz) mustard greens (*choy sum*)

The womenfolk in my family thought the world of this dish. This was especially so in the case of our laundry amah who spent several hours a day squatting in the wash area washing our clothes. Whenever my father cooked this dish, he always advised her to eat more of it.

Why? Because the heaty prawns and shrimp roe combined with the neutral fish maw and other nutritious ingredients produced a dish which we believed to strengthen the kidneys and the knee joints. The fact that the laundry amah took my father's advice and worked for us till a ripe old age must indicate the efficacy of the dish.

PRAWN PASTE SEASONING
1 teaspoon salt
1 teaspoon sugar
½ teaspoon light soya sauce
½ tablespoon cornflour
½ egg white
Dash of pepper

SUPERIOR STOCK
200 g (7 oz) chicken leg
100 g (3.5 oz) pork ribs
10 g (0.3 oz) Chinese ham
1.9 litres (7½ cups) hot water

FOR SCALDING FRIED FISH MAWS
1 litre (4 cups)
20 g (0.7 oz) spring onion
2 slices old ginger
1 teaspoon Chinese rice wine

FOR BLANCHING MUSTARD GREENS
1 litre (4 cups)
½ teaspoon salt
1 teaspoon oil

SAUCE
3 tablespoons cornflour
6 tablespoons water
½ tablespoon oyster sauce

Soak fried fish maws in water for 15 minutes. Cut fish maws into half lengthwise and then cut each length into 5 cm (2 inch) sections.

Bring scalding solution to a boil. Add in cut fish maws and boil for 2 minutes. Rinse and squeeze off excess water. Discard scalding solution.

Prepare superior stock. Scald all ingredients in 1 litre (4 cups) hot water for 2 minutes. Discard scalding liquid. Bring another 900 ml of water to a boil. Add in all scalded ingredients and simmer stock for 1 hour until 250 ml (1 cup) liquid is left. Sieve stock for later use.

Prepare prawn paste. Shell and devein prawns. Using the flat of a cleaver to flatten prawns on a chopping board. Chop finely. Put shrimps into a mixing bowl and add in the seasoning. Mix well and throw handfuls of the mixture against the bowl till it becomes a springy paste.

Sprinkle each piece of fish maw with a little cornflour and spread 1 tablespoon of prawn paste on it. Put the stuffed fish maws on a steaming plate and steam for 5 minutes. Blanch the mustard greens for 2 minutes and drain. When the fish maws are done, drain off steamed liquid and place on serving plate.

Garnish serving plate with blanched mustard greens. Bring superior stock to a boil. Add in cornflour solution to the boiling stock and stir for 1 minute to thicken. Pour sauce over steamed fish maws. Sprinkle shrimp roe over fish maws and serve immediately.

雲南汽鍋雞 ●

The Yunnan steam pot orginated from the district of Kean Sui Geng 建水景 in China's Yunnan province.

I was just twelve years old when I first saw a Yunnan steam pot. It was sold to my grandmother by a sailor who did not explain its use to her.

Nevertheless, my grandmother was fascinated with the smoothness of the clay and the unusual funnel which protruded into the pot. It could not be a vase, she said, because it has a cover. So she used the Yunnan pot to keep her jewellery. She even said that her jade would become more green because her special pot with the funnel would let fresh air in! That poor cooking pot served as her jewellery box for 16 years!

In 1973, I came to know the real use of the Yunnan pot when I was leafing though a copy of my husband's medical journals.

With the magazine in hand, I rushed to explain my 'discovery' to my grandmother. She quickly emptied the contents of her 'jewel pot' and after giving it a good scrub, we ventured to cook our first Yunnan pot dish. This was the recipe we used.

Grandmother liked the soup, but I loved the pot! Knowing my interest in cookery, she agreed to part with her precious pot on one condition – that I must NOT use it too often in case I should break it.

I have kept my word, and when the pot is not in use, it sits proudly in a showcase with my other antiques. I have bought several other Yunnan pots since then, but no other is better than my grandmother's 30-year-old Yunnan pot!

CHICKEN STEAMED IN YUNNAN POT

1 medium chicken (1.5 kg, 3.3 lb)
12 dried Chinese mushrooms
2 slices old ginger
1 tablespoon Chinese rice wine
1 litre (4½ cups) warm water
1.3 litres (5 cups) hot water
50 g Yunnan ham
2 stalks spring onion

SEASONING

1 teaspoon salt
1 teaspoon light soya sauce

Trim mushroom stems. Wash and soak mushrooms in 1 litre (4 cups) warm water for ½ hour.

Clean, gut and wash chicken. Trim off excess fat and cut into serving pieces. Scald in 625 ml (2½ cups) hot water for 1 minute. Rinse and drain. Trim fat from Yunnan ham. Scald the ham in 250 ml (1 cup) hot water for 1 minute. Rinse and drain. Cut into thick slices.

Clean, wash and cut spring onions into 5 cm (2 in) sections.

Put mushroom water and all ingredients except seasoning and Chinese rice wine into a Yunnan pot. Add another 375 ml (1½ cups) hot water.

Put lid on and place the Yunnan pot on a tripod over a wok of boiling water and steam for 2 hours over medium heat.

Add seasoning and the Chinese rice wine. Serve hot in the Yunnan pot. Complement with a small plate of light soya sauce.

STEAMED STUFFED MUSHROOMS

蒸釀冬菇

This is a very light and non-greasy dish suitable for both young and old. My father favoured it at festive meals.

The minced pork and prawn paste, with the addition of water chestnuts, makes an interesting texture which is pleasant to the bite. At the same time, these ingredients enhance the sweetness of Chinese mushrooms.

12 dried Chinese mushrooms
300 g (10.6 oz) prawns
100 g (3.5 oz) minced lean pork
3 water chestnuts
½ egg white
10 g (0.3 oz) spring onion, chopped finely
10 g (0.3 oz) coriander leaves, chopped finely
300 ml (1¼ cup) warm water

SEASONING
1 teaspoon salt
1 teaspoon sugar
1 teaspoon light soya sauce
½ tablespoon cornflour
Dash of pepper

CORNFLOUR THICKENING
1 tablespoon cornflour
2 tablespoons water

SAUCE
185 ml (¾ cup) reserved mushroom water
½ teaspoon salt
½ teaspoon sugar
½ tablespoon oyster sauce
½ teaspoon dark soya sauce

Trim stems from mushrooms. Soak mushroom in 250 ml (1 cup) warm water for ½ hour. Squeeze off excess water and retain mushroom water for stock.

Shell and devein prawns. Chop finely and mix well with the minced pork to make a paste. Add in the seasoning.

Wash and skin water chestnuts. Dice finely and add it to the paste. Include chopped spring onions and coriander leaves. Mix well.

Dust the underside of mushrooms lightly with a little cornflour. Spread paste evenly in each mushroom and smooth the top with a little cornflour thickening.

Place the stuffed mushrooms onto a steaming plate and steam over medium heat for 10 minutes. Remove and drain off excess water. Place steamed mushrooms on serving plate.

Bring 185 ml (¾ cup) of the reserved mushroom water and the rest of sauce ingredients to a boil for 5 minutes. Include the cornflour thickening and stir for 1 minute. Pour the sauce over steamed mushrooms and serve immediately.

小
盅
鷄
飯
○

STEAMED CHICKEN RICE IN SERVING CUPS

300 g (10.5 oz) raw rice
300 g (10.5 oz) chicken fillet
4 dried Chinese mushrooms
1 Chinese waxed sausage
10 g (0.3 oz) spring onion
10 g (0.3 oz) coriander leaves
1 red chilli, deseeded and sliced finely
185 ml (¾ cup) water
½ teaspoon salt
½ teaspoon sugar

MARINADE FOR CHICKEN
½ teaspoon salt
½ teaspoon sugar
1 teaspoon light soya sauce
1 teaspoon dark soya sauce
1 teaspoon ginger juice
1 teaspoon Chinese rice wine
½ tablespoon oyster sauce
1 tablespoon oil

SAUCE
1 teaspoon light soya sauce
1 teaspoon dark soya sauce
1 tablespoon oil

If you feel that bringing the whole claypot of rice to the dining table is not your cup of tea, try this recipe.

Here, the rice is prepared in individual serving cups so that each guest can be presented with his or her own steaming bowl of fragrant rice. No wonder this colourful and delicious dish is perfect for entertaining in the cool season.

The Chinese sausage and rice wine in the recipe act to whet the appetite.

Remove stem from mushrooms and soak in 185 ml (¾ cup) water for 15 minute. Squeeze off excess water and reserve water. Slice mushroom finely.

Wash and slice sausage at a slant. Wash rice and add to it ½ teaspoon each of salt and sugar.

Wash chicken fillet and drain. Slice finely and marinate with seasoning for 10 minutes. Add mushroom and sausage to marinated chicken and mix well. Divide mixture into four portions and place each portion in a small bowl.

Add 4 tablespoons of rice and 8 tablespoons mushroom water into each bowl. Cover bowls and steam for 30 minutes over high heat.

Unmould onto a serving plate and pour sauce over steamed rice. Garnish with spring onions, coriander leaves and red chilli before serving. Serve immediately.

釀
冬
瓜
●

CROWN OF GLORY

1 small winter melon (*tung kwa*) about 1 kg or 2.2 lb
40 g (1.4 oz) barley, boiled for 15 minutes and drained
40 g (1.4 oz) lotus seeds, boiled for 20 minutes and skinned
40 g (1.4 oz) gingko nuts, shelled
100 g (3.5 oz) chestnuts, shelled and boiled for 15 minutes,
    membrane removed
20 g (0.7 oz) medlar seeds, rinsed
20 g (0.7 oz) dried scallops, rinsed
200 g (7 oz) steamed crab meat
2 slices old ginger
1 teaspoon salt
1 tablespoon oil

The winter melon, contrary to its name, is a common summer vegetable. The Chinese love the melon for its cooling and refreshing effects.

If you do not like diced winter melon in soup, perhaps this stuffed melon dish will change your mind about the vegetable. It is said to be good for increasing appetite and especially beneficial when eaten during the hot season.

CHICKEN STOCK
200g (7 oz) chicken leg
100g (3.5 oz) lean pork
1.1 litres (4½ cups) water

CORNFLOUR THICKENING
1 tablespoon cornflour,
2 tablespoons water

SAUCE
375 ml (1½ cups) chicken stock
½ teaspoon salt
½ teaspoon sugar
1 tablespoon oyster sauce

Simmer ingredients for chicken stock for 1 hour or until reduced to 375 ml (1½ cups) stock. Peel winter melon. Slice off ⅓ from the top of the melon. Scoop out melon flesh to form a bowl about 1 inch all around. Wash and drain melon. Place melon in a steaming bowl.

Heat a wok with 1 tablespoon oil until smoky. Add ginger slices and fry for ½ minute. Add barley, lotus seeds, gingko nuts, chestnuts, medlar seeds, scallops and crab meat, and stir-fry for 5 minutes. Season with 1 teaspoon salt.

Place stir-fried stuffing into the hollow of the melon. Then place melon into the steamer with the stuffing end up and steam over medium heat for 2 hours. Remove melon and pour off excess water.

Place a serving platter over the mouth of the melon. Turn the melon over on the platter, carefully retaining any stock to be used as part of sauce.

To prepare the sauce, bring the 375 ml (1½ cups) of the chicken stock to a boil. Add in the remaining sauce ingredients to taste and boil slowly for 2 minutes. Include the cornflour thickening and stir well for 1 minute. Pour this hot sauce over the melon and serve immediately.

At the dining table, use a knife and cut the melon into wedges. Serve a wedge of melon and some stuffing together with sauce.

雪
山
鳳
凰
○

PHOENIX OF THE SNOW MOUNTAIN

1 large chicken (2 kg, 4.4 lb)
20 g (0.75 oz) spring onion
10 g (0.3 oz) old ginger slices
1 large fresh stawberry

MARINADE FOR CHICKEN	FOR EGG WHITE CUSTARD
185 ml (¾ cup) Chinese rice wine	3 egg whites
125 ml (½ cup) ginger juice	185 ml (¾ cup) fresh milk
40g (1.3 oz) salt	½ teaspoon salt

You must not let the name of this recipe or the appearance of the dish fool you. The main ingredient is only chicken and the plainess of the presentation belies its rich flavours.

Try to follow the recipe closely and you may feel a 'warm current' running through you after you have eaten this dish. This 'warm current' is how the Chinese express the effect of improved blood circulation through fortifying the stomach.

Clean and gut chicken. Wash thoroughly and drain.

Rub the inside and outside of the chicken with the marinade. Stuff the spring onions and ginger slices into the chicken and secure the opening with a toothpick. Leave chicken to marinade for 2 hours.

Steam the marinated chicken over medium flame for 30 minutes. Cool and debone chicken and cut meat into serving pieces. Discard ginger and spring onions but reserve steamed chicken stock for other recipes. Arrange chicken pieces on large serving platter.

Put egg whites in a large bowl. Add in the salt and use chopsticks to beat egg whites for 2 minutes until foamy. Include the milk and mix lightly. Pour egg white mixture slowly over chicken until it is completely covered. Steam over low flame for 10 minutes until egg whites become a custard.

Wash and dry strawberry. Place strawberry in the centre of the dish just before serving. Serve immediately.

清
蒸
鯧
魚
☯

STEAMED POMFRET

1 pomfret (about 600 g, 1.3 lb)
4 red dates (*hung choe*)
2 dried mushrooms
20 g (0.75 oz) spring onion
20 g (0.75 oz) coriander leaves
2 slices old ginger
185 ml (⅔ cup) water

SEASONING
1 teaspoon salt
½ teaspoon sugar
1 teaspoon light soya sauce
½ teaspoon dark soya sauce
1 tablespoon oil
Dash of pepper

You may not believe me, but I assure you that I was 'forced' to eat two small pomfrets per day for two years after a kidney ailment.

Why such a fishy deal? Because my father insisted that pomfrets, of all fishes, are the choicest and that they have the effect of reinforcing the 'chi' or vital life force in the body.

Surprisingly, I still enjoy eating pomfret as I love its smooth skin and delicate taste and texture.

Remove the stems and soak mushrooms in 150 ml (¾ cup) water for 15 minutes. Squeeze off excess water and discard. Slice mushrooms finely.

Remove stones from red dates. Wash and tear dates into small pieces.

Wash and shred spring onion and coriander leaves finely.

Remove gills and gut pomfret. Wash and drain.

Rub 1 teaspoon salt and ½ teaspoon sugar inside and outside of the fish. Put fish on a shallow dish and pour on the light and dark soya sauce and oil. Sprinkle on mushrooms, red dates and ginger.

Steam fish over high flame for 10 minutes.

Garnish with spring onion and coriander leaves. Add a dash of pepper and serve immediately.

The southern Chinese have always favoured waxed sausages and waxed bacon during the winter months. As the cold season approaches, it is common to see families preparing or stocking up these items. My grandmother used to keep the habit of buying these products around the Lunar New Year although we were living in tropical Singapore.

Waxed products get their glossy wax-like coating from having been soaked in oil as a preservative. Waxed sausages are made from sesasoned minced pork or liver stuffed, with some fat, into sausage skins. These skins are literally known to the Chinese as 'intestinal clothing' 肠衣.

Waxed bacon, made from streaky pork with layers of skin, fat and lean meat is another popular waxed product. These products are traditionally wind dried 风乾 in the late autumn.

腊味飯

○

STEAMED RICE WITH CHINESE SAUSAGE AND BACON

1 pair Chinese waxed pork sausage (*larp cheong*)
1 pair Chinese waxed liver sausage (*yuen cheong*)
300 g (10.6 oz) Chinese waxed bacon (*larp yok*)
6 dried Chinese mushrooms

RICE MIXTURE
2 cups uncooked rice
1 teaspoon salt
1.5 litres (6 cups) water

Trim mushroom stems and soak mushrooms in 375 ml (1½ cups) water. Squeeze off excess water and retain the mushroom water. Slice mushrooms coarsely.

Wash and scald bacon in hot water for 1 minute to remove excess oil. Drain and slice thickly. Wash and dry sausages.

Wash rice and put into a claypot. Season with 1 teaspoon salt. Pour in the reserved mushroom water and add remaining water to make a total of 1.5 litres (6 cups). Spread the sausages and sliced mushrooms on top of the rice.

Cover claypot and bring to a boil. When the liquid begins to subside, spread bacon on top of the rice. Leave to cook over low heat for 15 minutes until the rice is done.

Remove sausages from the rice and cut into thick slices. Return sliced sausages to the claypot and stir well into rice. Leave the mixture for 5 minutes before serving in the claypot for an authentic touch.

YUNNAN HERBAL CHICKEN SOUP

淮杞汽鍋鷄 ○

1 medium chicken (1.5 kg, 3.3lb)
10 g (0.3 oz) longan flesh
30 g (1 oz) dioscorea (*wai san*)
20 g (0.7 oz) medlar seeds (*kei chee*)
8 dried Chinese mushrooms
1.75 litres (7 cups) hot water

SEASONING
1 teaspoon salt
1 teaspoon light soya sauce

Trim mushroom stems. Wash and soak mushrooms in 750 ml (3 cups) warm water for ½ hour. Retain mushroom water.

Clean, gut, and wash chicken. Cut chicken into 8 pieces. Scald chicken in 625 ml (2½ cups) hot water for 2 minutes. Rinse and drain.

Rinse longan flesh, dioscorea and medlar seeds briefly.

Put all the herbs, chicken, and mushrooms and mushroom water into the Yunnan pot. Pour in 1.1 litres (4½ cups) hot water.

Cover lid and place the Yunnan pot on a tripod over a wok of boiling water. Steam for 3 hours over medium heat.

Add seasoning before serving. Serve soup hot in Yunnan pot.

The Yunnan pot is used here to prepare a rich chicken herbal tonic. However, it can also be used to steam a light tasty dish. Simply season some meat and seafood and steam over high heat for 10-15 minutes.

STEAMED MILK WITH GINGER JUICE

姜汁奶 ○

White from an egg
3 half egg-shells of fresh milk
2 tablespoons castor sugar
½ teaspoon ginger juice

Add sugar and milk to egg white. Beat for 2 minutes until mixture is slightly creamy.

Put in ginger juice and mix well.

Pour mixture into steaming bowl and skim bubbles, if any.

Steam over high flame for 5 minutes and then lower heat and steam for another 10 minutes. Serve hot or chilled.

Some people have the habit of drinking a glass of warm milk before going to bed; my nanny thought likewise, but she fancied a milk custard instead.

As a child, I was given this custard once or twice a month so much so that I asked why I had to eat it all the time. I was only told, "It's good for you."

My research later revealed that warm milk has the effect of soothing the nerves and ginger juice is added to alleviate 'wind' from the body.

The Chinese have their tried and true method of measuring liquid for making custard: by using the shells of the eggs used. The ratio is one egg to three half egg-shells of liquid.

蒸
猪
腦
○

STEAMED PIG'S BRAIN

4 sets pig's brain
4 dried Chinese mushrooms, stems removed
3 red dates (hung choe)
80 g (3 oz) minced lean pork
125 ml (½ cup) water

SEASONING FOR PIG'S BRAIN	MARINADE FOR PORK
1 teaspoon salt	1 teaspoon salt
1 teaspoon sugar	1 teaspoon sugar
Dash of pepper	½ teaspoon light soya sauce
1 tablespoon Chinese rice wine	1 tablespoon cornflour
1 tablespoon ginger juice	
1 tablespoon oil	

My friends have always complimented me on my good memory. For this I have to give credit to my diet of pig's brain.

This dish is reputed to have the effect of fortifying memory. Don't worry about cholesterol – Chinese believe that you must try to eat a little of everything to balance your body complex. So why not start right from the top?

Remove red veins from pig's brain with a toothpick. Rinse and drain. Add in seasoning and mash lightly.

Soak mushrooms in 125 ml (½ cup) water for 15 minutes. Squeeze off excess water and slice finely. Remove seeds from red dates. Wash and slice finely.

Marinade minced pork for 10 minutes. Add in mushrooms and red dates.

Place the mixture on a steaming plate. Spread the seasoned pig's brain on top of meat. Steam over high heat for over 15 minutes. Serve hot.

NOTE: *Each set of pig's brain consists of 3 parts.*

豆
腐
蒸
蛋
◑

STEAMED BEANCURD CUSTARD

500 g (1 lb) soft beancurd
50 g (1.75 oz) Chinese ham, chopped
2 eggs
10 g (0.3 oz) spring onions, chopped
10 g (0.3 oz) coriander leaves, chopped
6 half egg shells of water
1 teaspoon oil

Cured ham is one of the favourite delicacies of the Chinese. In olden days, these preserved meats were a real luxury available only to the nobility.

My father favoured the Kumhua ham from Chekiang province which he found to be superior in flavour to Yunnan ham. Kumhua ham has thick, golden skin with more lean meat than fat and has a refreshing salty tang. Yunnan ham, on the other hand, has thin, pale skin with more fat than lean meat. It is also sweeter and less salty than the Kumhua variety.

Although Chinese ham has little health-giving properties, it is the Number One flavouring for bland ingredients.

This delicious and easily digestible dish is one of my favourites.

魚
肉
蒸
蛋

This is a very popular custard which is suitable for both young and old as both fish and eggs are high in protein.

SEASONING

1 teaspoon salt
1 teaspoon sugar

SAUCE

1 teaspoon light soya sauce
1 teaspoon dark soya sauce
1 tablespoon oil

Break eggs into a large bowl. Add in seasoning and 6 half egg-shells of water. Beat lightly for 1 minute. Mash beancurd coarsely and add into the beaten eggs. Then added chopped ham and mix well.

Oil a steaming dish with 1 teaspoon oil and pour the beancurd mixture into it. Spread evenly. Steam over high flame for 5 minutes and then turn heat to low and continue to steam for another 10 minutes.

Pour sauce over custard and garnish with chopped spring onion and coriander leaves before serving.

STEAMED FISH CUSTARD

300 g (10.5 oz) fillet of white fish
2 eggs
10 g (0.3 oz) spring onion
10 g (0.3 oz) coriander leaves
6 half egg shells of water
1 teaspoon oil

SEASONING

1 teaspoon salt
1 teaspoon sugar
1 teaspoon light soya sauce

SAUCE

½ teaspoon dark soya sauce
1 tablespoon oil

Wash and chop spring onion and coriander leaves.

Break eggs into a large bowl. Add in seasoning and 6 half egg-shells of water. Beat with chopsticks lightly for 1 minute. Spread 1 teaspoon oil on a steaming dish and pour in the egg mixture.

Cut fish fillet into 3 cm (1½ inch) cubes and put into beaten egg mixture evenly. Steam mixture for 5 minutes over high flame then turn heat to low and continue to steam for another 10 minutes.

Pour sauce over custard and garnish with chopped spring onion and coriander leaves before serving.

麒
麟
班
片
☯

STEAMED FISH FILLET
WITH MUSHROOM AND HAM

300 g (10.5 oz) white fish fillet (grouper)
8 dried Chinese mushrooms
50 g (1.75 oz) Chinese ham
300 g (10.6 oz) mustard greens (choy sum)
10 g (0.3 oz) spring onion, shred finely
10 g (0.3 oz) coriander leaves, shred finely

SEASONING FOR FISH
1 teaspoon salt
1 teaspoon sugar
Dash of pepper
½ teaspoon light soya sauce
½ teaspoon oyster sauce
½ teaspoon ginger juice
1 tablespoon oil

FOR BLANCHING MUSTARD GREENS
1 litre (4 cups) boiling water
1 teaspoon salt
1 teaspoon oil

My father, who had vast experience as a chef, told me that timing is vital for steamed dishes. This is because steamed dishes should be served the moment they are ready; any delay would result in a less than satisfactory taste and presentation.

You can turn this to your advantage when you are entertaining at home. Since cooking time required for steaming is often short, your guests will wonder what magic you possess when you disappear into the kitchen for only a few moments and reappear with a beautifully garnished, steaming hot dish.

Your secret is, of course, the fact that you have prepared all the ingredients well in advance and that you have a pot of boiling water standing by for steaming the dish.

Remove stems and soak mushroom in water for 15 minutes. Squeeze off excess water.

Cut fish fillet into thick slices. Marinate with seasoning for 5 minutes.

Cut Chinese ham into thin slices.

Arrange the sliced ham, fish and mushrooms alternately in two rows on a steaming plate. Pour the excess marinade over the ingredients. Steam for 5 minutes over high flame.

Wash and blanch the mustard greens in the blaching solution for 2 minutes. Drain the vegetables well.

Garnish the steamed ingredients with the blanched vegetables, shredded spring onion and coriander leaves. Serve hot.

冬
菇
蒸
鷄
○

STEAMED CHICKEN WITH MUSHROOMS

½ small chicken (0.5 kg, 1 lb)
4 dried Chinese mushrooms
2 Chinese waxed sausages
185 ml (¾ cup) water

MARINADE
1 teaspoon salt
1 teaspoon sugar
1 teaspoon light soya sauce
1 teaspoon dark soya sauce
1 tablespoon ginger juice
1 tablespoon Chinese rice wine
1 tablespoon oyster sauce
1 tablespoon cornflour
1 tablespoon oil

This is one of the first dishes that I mastered from my mother. Her recipe used the ordinary steaming method, but when I discovered that a Yunnan pot made the ingredients more tender, I adapted the original recipe for the Yunnan pot. The result is no less authentic.

This nourishing dish is reputed by the Chinese to improve blood circulation.

Soak mushrooms in 185 ml (¾ cup) water for 30 minutes. Squeeze out excess water and and retain mushroom water. Slice the mushrooms thinly.

Clean chicken and cut into serving pieces. Marinate chicken for 15 minutes. Rinse sausages and slice thinly.

Add sausage, mushrooms and mushroom water to marinated chicken. Mix well. Put food into a Yunnan steam pot, cover lid and place the pot on a tripod in a big wok. The water level should be 5 cm (2 inches) away from the base of the pot. Steam for 15 minutes over high flame.

Serve hot in the Yunnan pot.

STEAMED LIVER
& FUNGI IN YUNNAN POT

雙耳蒸豬膶 ○

400 g (14 oz) pig's liver
10 g (0.3 oz) cloud fungus (*wan yee*)
10 g (0.3 oz) snow fungus (*shuet yee*)
10 g (0.3 oz) dried lily buds (*kum chum*)
3 slices old ginger
100 g (3.5 oz) spring onion

MARINADE FOR LIVER
1 teaspoon salt
1 teaspoon sugar
1 teaspoon light soya sauce
½ teaspoon dark soya sauce
1 tablespoon cornflour
1 tablespoon Chinese rice wine
1 tablespoon ginger juice
1 tablespoon oyster sauce
2 tablespoons oil

This is one of the many dishes which my grandmother cooked for me after I had been ill. She said this dish is good for improving blood circulation and stimulating appetite.

My research has proven her advice to be true since cloud and snow fungi are said to strengthen the lungs while dried lily buds and liver are high in iron and other metallic elements important to a convalescent.

Soak cloud and snow fungus in water for 30 minutes. Remove stems and grit. Tear into florets. Rinse and drain.

Knot each dried lily bud and soak them in water for 10 minutes. Rinse and squeeze off excess water. Set aside.

Wash and cut liver into thick slices across the grain. Marinate with seasoning for 10 minutes.

Combine cloud and snow fungus, lily buds, ginger and spring onion with marinated liver.

Pour mixture into Yunnan pot. Cover lid and place pot on tripod in a big wok. The water level should be 5 cm (2 inches) away from the base of the pot.

Steam for 7 to 10 minutes over high heat and serve immediately. The liver should not be overcooked.

Serve food in the Yunnan pot for an authentic touch.

荷
葉
蒸
田
鷄
●

The Chinese have a liking for frogs. Before they were bred for the dining table, edible frogs (Rana Nigromaculata) were mostly found in padi fields. They taste like chicken, but the flesh is more tender, being superior to chicken in texture. No wonder edible frogs are known in Chinese as 'Padi Field Chickens' 田鸡. This was one of my father's favourite dishes. If you cannot get hold of fresh lotus leaves, you can use dried ones which are available from Chinese medical shops.

This is a very refreshing dish for the hot season.

FROG STEAMED IN LOTUS LEAF

2 dried lotus leaves
8 frogs *(teen kai)*
10 g (0.3 oz) Chinese ham (see page 86)
6 dried Chinese mushrooms, discard stems
200 g (7 oz) carrot, skinned and sliced
20 g (0.75 oz) spring onions, cut into 5 cm (2 inch) lengths

MARINADE FOR FROG
1 teaspoon salt
1 teaspoon sugar
1 teaspoon light soya sauce
1 tablespoon cornflour
1 tablespoon Chinese rice wine
1 tablespoon ginger juice
½ teaspoon dark soya sauce
1 tablespoon oil

Soak the dried lotus leaves in warm water for 30 minutes. Wash and dry leaves with a towel. Set aside.

Clean and wash frogs thoroughly. Cut frogs into serving pieces. Marinate for 10 minutes.

Remove stems and soak the mushrooms in water. Squeeze off and discard excess water. Slice the mushrooms.

Shred Chinese ham coarsely.

Add sliced mushrooms, Chinese ham, carrot and spring onions to marinated frogs just before cooking. Mix well.

Place marinated frogs in the centre of lotus leaves. Wrap up into a package and place folded side down in a big bowl. Steam for 20 minutes over high heat.

Place lotus leaf packet on a serving plate. Use kitchen scissors to cut a big cross at the top of the packet and pull the flaps back. Serve hot.

NOTE: *Frogs are available from wet markets and prepared frog parts can be found in supermarkets. Dried lotus leaves are available from Chinese medical halls.*

清蒸笋壳 ☯

STEAMED MARBLE GOBE

This brownish-black freshwater fish has tasty, pure white flesh. I prefer the smaller Malayan species commonly found in tin mining pools to the larger Indo-Chinese species because the smaller fish have better texture.

Marble Gobes must be cooked as soon as they are killed to maintain the springy texture of the flesh. This is why the Chinese only purchase live Marble Gobes from the market and prepare them at home.

This dish is said to be good for convalescents as the fish is believed to stimulate the appetite.

1 Marble Gobe, about 600 g (1.3 lb) *(soon hock)*
3 slices of old ginger, shred finely
20 g (0.75 oz) spring onion, shred finely
20 g (0.75 oz) coriander leaves, shred finely
500 ml (2 cups) hot water

SEASONING
1 teaspoon salt
1 teaspoon light soya sauce
1 teaspoon dark soya sauce
1 tablespoon oil
Dash of pepper
½ teaspoon Chinese rice wine

Scale, gut and clean fish thoroughly. Scald with hot water for 30 seconds to remove the slime on the fish. Rinse and pat dry.

Rub salt over fish. Add in light and dark soya sauce and oil. Sprinkle shredded ginger over fish. Steam fish over high flame for 10 minutes.

Switch off heat and add in pepper and Chinese rice wine. Garnish with spring onion and coriander leaves. Serve immediately.

NOTE: *Choose a live fish and have the fishmonger prepare it for you. For best efficacy, cook the fish as soon as possible.*

蒸比目魚 ☯

STEAMED SOLE

1 tablespoon oil 1 sole (about 800g, 1.8 lb)
6 red dates *(hung choe)*
3 dried Chinese mushrooms
100 g (3.5 oz) lean pork
10 g (0.3 oz) spring onion, shred finely
10 g (0.3 oz) coriander leaves, shred finely
2 slices old ginger, shred finely

SEASONING FOR FISH
1 teaspoon sugar
1 teaspoon light soya sauce
½ teaspoon dark soya sauce
1 tablespoon oil
Dash of pepper

MARINADE FOR PORK
¼ teaspoon light soya sauce
¼ teaspoon sugar
1 teaspoon oil

This recipe was created by my husband. He mastered it when he was a student in England where soles are common.

Red dates and mushrooms are added to enhance the flavour of the fish. My children love it, but were surprised to find that this fish has flesh on only one side.

Scale sole. Clean and gut fish thoroughly. Remove skin if preferred.

Remove stems from mushrooms and soak mushrooms in water for 15 minutes. Squeeze off excess water and discard. Slice mushrooms thinly.

Wash red dates and remove stones. Tear into small pieces.

Rinse and dry lean pork. Shred finely and marinate for 5 minutes.

Rub seasoning over fish and place it on a steaming dish. Arrange lean pork, mushroom, red dates and ginger on top of fish. Steam for 10 minutes over high flame.

Garnish with shredded spring onion and coriander leaves just before serving. Serve hot.

三黃蛋

STEAMED VARIETY EGGS

1 Chinese century egg (*pei tan*)
1 Chinese salted egg (*hum tan*)
2 eggs
20 g (0.75 oz) coriander leaves, chopped
20 g (0.75 oz) spring onion, chopped
6 half egg shells of water
½ tablespoon oil

SEASONING
½ teaspoon salt
½ tablespoon oil
½ teaspoon dark soya sauce

My grandmother told me that this is a very traditional egg custard reputed to have the effect of "pushing out the dirty things from the body." She also said that it was good for "opening the mouth of the stomach."

What she meant was century eggs have the effect of removing impurities in the blood stream while salted eggs help in driving out latent heat. And, of course, once your body's system is clear of toxic elements, you will naturally have a good appetite.

Remove the black soil covering the salted egg. Rinse and break salted egg into a small container. Separate the yolk from the white. Dice the raw yolk finely and put aside. Reserve white.

Wash and shell century egg. Dice the whole egg coarsely.

Break the eggs into a big container. Add in the salted egg whites and 6 half egg-shells water.

Add ½ teaspoon salt and beat the egg and salted egg white with chopsticks for 1 minute until mixture is a bit creamy. Add in the diced yolk and century egg.

Brush a shallow steaming dish with ½ tablespoon oil. Pour the egg mixture into the oiled container and steam for 5 minutes over high flame. Turn heat to low and continue to steam for another 10 minutes.

Pour ½ tablespoon oil and ½ teaspoon dark soya sauce over the steamed custard. Garnish with chopped coriander leaves and spring onion. Serve hot.

蒜茸蒸蝦 ○

STEAMED MINCED GARLIC PRAWNS

500 g (1.1 lb) large prawns
20 g (0.75 oz) spring onion, chopped
20 g (0.75 oz) coriander leaves, chopped
1 red chilli, deseeded and chopped finely

SEASONING
4 cloves garlic
2 shallots
2 slices old ginger
1 tablespoon fermented black beans (*dao si*)
1 teaspoon salt
1 teaspoon sugar
2 tablespoons oil
1 teaspoon Chinese rice wine

The Chinese classify prawns as a food which stimulates the 'yang' essence of the body. They say it brings 'warmth' to vital organs like the kidneys and thus strengthens them.

Prawns, however, are not aphrodisiacs which some believe them to be.

The minced garlic used here reinforces the 'warming' effect of the prawns while fermented black beans simply enhance the taste of the dish.

Trim off the feelers and legs of the prawns. Rinse and pat dry. Use a sharp knife and slice each prawn in half, lengthwise down the back. Remove black veins.

Mince garlic, shallots and ginger finely.

Rinse fermented black beans and chop finely. Add to garlic mixture.

Add salt, sugar and oil to this mixture. Mix well and marinate prawns with this for 5 minutes.

Place prawns, shell down on a shallow container and steam over high heat for 5 minutes.

Sprinkle with Chinese rice wine and garnish with coriander leaves, spring onion and red chilli before serving. Serve immediately.

荷葉飯 ☯

STEAMED RICE IN LOTUS LEAF

2 cups uncooked rice
200 g (7 oz) chicken fillet
200 g (7 oz) barbecued pork (char siew)
4 dried mushrooms
200 g (7 oz) prawns
1 Chinese waxed sausage (larp cheong)
1 egg
1 dried lotus leaf
2 tablespoons oil

SEASONING
2½ teaspoon salt
2 teaspoon sugar
1 teaspoon light soya sauce
1 teaspoon oil

This is one of the popular Southern Chinese rice dishes usually served during the hot season.

You may wish to make smaller packets of lotus rice by cutting each lotus leaf into quarters. These miniature packets can be served as dim sum items.

Wash and put rice in rice cooker. Add in 1.3 litres (5 cups) water and bring to a boil for 10 minutes. Lower heat and continue to cook for 10 minutes over low heat. Leave to cool.

Soak the lotus leaf in hot water for 30 minutes. Wipe dry and set aside for later use. Beat egg with ½ teaspoon salt.

Trim stems from mushrooms and soak in water for 15 minutes. Squeeze off excess water and dice mushroom coarsely. Discard mushroom water. Shell and devein shrimps. Dice coarsely and marinate in ½ teaspoon each of salt, sugar and oil for 5 minutes.

Wash and dry chicken fillet. Dice coarsely and marinate in ½ teaspoon each of salt, sugar and oil for 5 minutes. Rinse and dice sausage coarsely.

Heat 1 tablespoon oil in a wok until smoky. Put in the marinated prawns and chicken and stir-fry for 1 minute. Remove from wok. Heat wok again and add in 1 tablespoon oil and heat till smoky. Pour in the beaten egg and fry well for 1 minute until partly golden. Remove from wok. Clean wok. Heat wok again until smoky and add in the diced sausages, barbecued pork and mushrooms. Fry well for 1 minute.

Add in the cooked rice and mix well. Include the remaining seasoning, then put in the cooked prawns, chicken and lastly the omelette. Fry all the ingredients for 2 minutes. Switch off the heat.

Spread the dry lotus leaf in the centre of a big bowl. Pour the cooked rice mixture onto the leaf and fold and tuck in the sides of the leaf to form a big square packet. Place the bowl with the lotus leaf packet in a bamboo steamer and steam over high heat for 25 minutes.

To serve, place packet in the centre of serving plate. Open the rice packet in front of guests so that they can smell the aroma of the lotus. Serve immediately.

NOTE: *Dried lotus leaves are available from Chinese medical halls.*

STEAMED WATER CHESTNUTS WITH MINCED MEAT

馬蹄蒸肉鬆 ●

200 g (7 oz) lean pork, minced
4 Chinese mushrooms
6 water chestnuts, peeled and diced finely
60 ml (¼ cup) warm water

SEASONING
1 teaspoon salt
1 teaspoon sugar
1 teaspoon light soya sauce
1 tablespoon cornflour

Remove mushroom stems and rinse mushrooms briefly. Soak mushrooms in 60 ml (¼ cup) of warm water for 15 minutes. Squeeze out excess water and reserve water for later use. Dice mushrooms finely.

Marinate minced pork with seasoning. Add diced water chestnuts and mushrooms to the minced pork and mix into a paste. Spread the mixture on a steaming plate and add mushroom water. Steam the mixture for 15 minutes over medium flame. Serve hot with plain rice.

Ancient Chinese medical texts record that water chestnuts are a good form of roughage, able to cleanse the intestinal tract of 'yang' elements.

I remember that when my youngest brother swallowed a coin when he was very young, his nanny immediately fed him a few fresh water chestnuts. She said that this was to get the coin out of his system, and it was effective.

So, if your children dislike vegetables, serve this dish for a change instead.

STEAMED EGG CUSTARD

冰花滑蛋

1 egg
3 half egg-shells of water
1½ teaspoons castor sugar
½ teaspoon ginger juice

Break egg into a bowl and add sugar and water. Beat mixture for 3 minutes until slightly creamy. Add ginger juice and mix well.

Pour mixture into a small steaming bowl. Skim bubbles from the top of the mixture, if any.

Steam over high flame for 5 minutes and then lower flame and continue to steam for another 10 minutes. Serve hot or chilled.

My mother has always believed that eggs have the effect of improving the complexion. I have to trust her judgement since she has the looks of a sixty-year-old even though she is well into her seventies. So, if you are looking for an economical dessert to help you look young, this recipe is for you!

枸杞蒸魚片 ○

STEAMED FISH SLICES WITH MEDLAR LEAVES

300 g (10.5 oz) threadfin or other white fish
10 g (0.3 oz) medlar seeds (*kei chee*)
40 g (1.5 oz) fresh medlar leaves (*kow kei*)

SEASONING
1 teaspoon salt
1 teaspoon sugar
1 tablespoon oyster sauce
1 tablespoon oil

Rinse medlar seeds briefly. Pluck medlar leaves and discard the stems. Wash and drain leaves. Wash and pat dry. Slice thinly and marinate with seasoning for 5 minutes.

Place the marinated fish slices in the centre of a porcelain plate and surround the fish with medlar leaves. Sprinkle medlar seeds on the fish. Steam for 5 minutes over high flame. Serve hot.

My nanny cooked this dish for me from the time I started school. My grandmother also used to tell my mother to prepare this dish for her quite regularly. You see, the Chinese believe that medlar seeds and medlar leaves improve eyesight and brighten the eyes.

The result for my grandmother was fantastic – she could do her sewing without spectacles even at the ripe old age of 80.

芫茜鷄腎

○

STEAMED SPICY CHICKEN GIZZARDS

8 chicken gizzards
2 stalks coriander leaves
1 teaspoon salt

SAUCE
2 teaspoons dark soya sauce
2 tablespoons oil
½ teaspoon sesame oil

SEASONING
2 teaspoons salt
2 teaspoons sugar
2 slices old ginger
2 stalks spring onion, cut into 5 cm (2 in) lengths
8 white peppercorns
2 small pieces cinnamon
2 pieces star anise
4 stem cloves
2 tablespoons Chinese rice wine
1 small piece tangerine peel
2 tablespoons water

Remove fat from chicken gizzards. Rub thoroughly with 1 teaspoon salt. Rinse and drain.

Mix seasoning in a bowl and add cleaned gizzards. Mix well.

Steam gizzards for 1 hour over medium flame. Remove gizzards and discard spicy stock.

Slice gizzards lengthwise thinly and garnish with coriander leaves.

Sprinkle sliced gizzards with sauce before serving.

Coriander leaf is regarded by the Chinese as a vegetable and a herb that possesses both nuitritional and medicinal qualities. The spicy gizzards in this recipe work as a catalyst on the coriander leaves to cleanse the palate and clear the internal organs of any toxic elements.

I personally look upon this recipe as a sure cure for bad breath!

荷葉蒸鷄 ☯

CHICKEN STEAMED IN LOTUS LEAF

½ medium chicken, about 750g (1.6 lb)
40 g (1.5 oz) medlar seeds (*kei chee*)
50 g (2 oz) precooked lotus seeds
2 slices old ginger
2 stalks spring onions, cut into 3 cm (1.5 inch) lengths
2 dried lotus leaves

MARINADE FOR CHICKEN
½ teaspoon salt
1 teaspoon sugar
1 teaspoon light soya sauce
2 tablespoons cornflour
1 tablespoon ginger juice
1 tablespoon Chinese rice wine
1 tablespoon oyster sauce
1 tablespoon oil

The lotus leaf, favoured as a fragrant wrapping for Chinese food, comes from the water lily family (Nelumbo Nucifera Gaertn). They are said to have a refreshing effect on the body system. This dish is believed to benefit the digestive tract and improve the eyesight.

Soak lotus leaves in warm water for about 30 minutes until soft. Wash and drain. Wipe dry and put aside.

Blanch lotus seeds in hot water for 5 minutes. Drain. Rinse and drain medlar seeds.

Clean and cut chicken into serving pieces. Marinate for 15 minutes. Add lotus seeds, medlar seeds, ginger and spring onions to chicken. Mix well.

Place cleaned lotus leaf in the centre of the plate. Put the chicken mixture in the centre and wrap up with the lotus leaf. Place the packet in a bowl and steam for 30 minutes on medium heat.

Switch off heat and wipe off evaporation in the steaming bowl.

Place the packet on a serving plate. Use scissors to cut a big hole in the centre of the lotus packet to expose cooked ingredients. Serve hot.

NOTE: *Dried lotus leaves are available from Chinese medical halls.*

銀
魚
仔
蒸
蛋
☯

STEAMED EGG CUSTARD
WITH WHITEBAIT

100 g (3.5 oz) cooked whitebait
3 eggs
2 slices old ginger
9 half egg shells of water
1 tablespoon oil

SEASONING
1 teaspoon salt
1 teaspoon light soya sauce
1 teaspoon sugar

SAUCE
1 tablespoon oil
½ teaspoon light soya sauce
½ teaspoon dark soya sauce

The Chinese eat the anchovy-like whitebait for the calcium it provides. Thus, this fish is eaten to stengthen bones.

Traditionally, these tiny fish are steamed with salt immediately after they are caught. They are left to cool in large, shallow trays before being offered for sale in markets.

Rinse and drain whitebait.

Break eggs into a bowl. Add in 1 teaspoon salt, 1 teaspoon light soya sauce and 9 half egg-shells of water. Beat well for 2 minutes.

Coat the inside of steaming plate with ½ tablespoon oil and pour in egg mixture.

Steam for 5 minutes over high flame and then lower flame to steam for another 10 minutes.

Heat ½ tablespoon oil in a wok. When the oil begins to smoke, put in ginger and fry till fragrant. Add whitebait and fry for 5 minutes. Finally, include 1 teaspoon sugar and fry until fishes are golden brown and crispy. Remove and cool.

When the custard is cooked, remove from the steamer and pour sauce over it. Sprinkle fried whitebait on custard just before serving.

NOTE: *Cooked whitebait is available at wet markets.*

醉鳳凰 DRUNKEN PHOENIX

○

1 medium chicken (1.5 kg, 3.3 lb)
3 stalks spring onion
2 slices old ginger

MARINADE
2 teaspoons salt
1 teaspoon light soya sauce
2 tablespoons Chinese rose wine (*mui gwei lo*)

GARNISH
2 stalks spring onion, shredded
1 red chilli, shredded

GINGER SAUCE
2 tablespoons grated ginger
1 teaspoon chopped spring onion
½ teaspoon salt
½ teaspoon sugar
2 tablespoons chicken stock from steamed chicken

OYSTER SAUCE
2 tablespoons oyster sauce
1 tablespoon chicken stock from steamed chicken
1 teaspoon chopped spring onion

My mother used this recipe when she prepared chicken as an offering during festivals and feast days. She emphasised that chicken cooked in this way will be tasty and delicious even after having been left on the offering table for a long time.

The Chinese rose wine used here is made from Kaoliang spirit, rose petals and sugar. It has a strong fragrance and a slightly sweet taste. It can be drunk as a liqueur or used to flavour marinades.

This Chinese rose wine will stimulate blood circulation and the ginger sauce serves to alleviate 'wind' from the body.

Gut chicken and wash thoroughly. Drain well. Marinate chicken (including cavity) for 15 minutes.

Stuff the spring onions and ginger slices into the cavity of chicken and seal opening with toothpicks.

Place chicken on a plate and steam for 20–30 minutes over high heat.

Remove toothpicks and discard spring onion and ginger. Retain chicken stock for making the ginger and oyster sauces.

Cut chicken into serving pieces and place neatly on a serving plate. Garnish with spring onion and red chilli. Serve with ginger and oyster sauces.

蒸發財魚
●

FISH STEAMED ON LOTUS LEAF

4 Trevally (*fatt choy yu*) or any small white fish
1 dried lotus leaf
1 piece preserved tangerine peel (5 g or 0.2 oz)
2 cloves garlic, chopped
2 slices old ginger, shredded
1 small red chilli, seeds removed and cut into rings
1 stalk spring onion, chopped
1 stalk coriander leaves, plucked

MARINADE FOR FISH
1 teaspoon salt
1 teaspoon sugar
1 teaspoon light soya sauce
2 tablespoons oil

Trevally is known as the Chinese New Year Fish or fatt choy yu, literally 'Prosperity Fish'.

Trevally spawn during the Chinese New Year season, and the fish is an auspicious ingredient for meals as the rich roe and creamy milt symbolize abundance and wealth.

The fish is available all year round although with little or no roe. In the Far East, the cost of the fish escalates up to more than ten times the usual price during the Chinese New Year period.

Wash and soak dried lotus leaf in warm water for 30 minutes. Drain and pat dry with kitchen towel. Line a large bamboo steamer with the lotus leaf. Trim excess leaf from edges.

Wash and soak preserved tangerine peel for 15 minutes. Chop finely.

Clean fishes. If you are using Trevally during the Chinese New year season, the fish will be heavy with roe, so do not slit open the stomach. Marinade the fishes.

Place the fishes on the lotus leaf in the steamer. Sprinkle tangerine peel, garlic and ginger on the fishes. Cover steamer and steam over high heat for 5 minutes or till fish are done.

Garnish with spring onion, coriander leaves and red chilli.

Serve immediately.

SEAFOOD IN YUNNAN POT

雲南海鮮鍋 ○

10 oysters, shelled and rinsed

10 medium prawns, shelled and deveined

1 squid (100 g, 3.5 oz), cleaned and cut into rings

200 g (7 oz) white fish fillet, sliced thickly

10 slices carrot

2 slices ginger

2 stalks spring onions, cut into 5 cm (2 in) sections

MARINADE FOR SEAFOOD

2 teaspoons salt

2 teaspoons sugar

1 teaspoon light soya sauce

½ teaspoon dark soya sauce

1 tablespoon cornflour

1 tablespoon oyster sauce

1 tablespoon oil

Dash of pepper

This is my own version of cooking seafood in a Yunnan pot. Seafood should never be overcooked and steaming it in a Yunnan pot cooks it just right.

If you are looking for a dish to reinforce your 'yang' essence, this may be the recipe for you.

Marinate all the seafood for 5 minutes. Add the ginger, spring onions and carrot to the marinated seafood. Mix well.

Put all the ingredients into a Yunnan pot. Cover lid and place pot on a tripod in a big wok. The water level should be 5 cm (2 inches) away from the base of the pot. Steam for 10 minutes over high heat.

Serve seafood hot in Yunnan pot.

SIMMERING

湯羹煲法

Simmer to gently coax out the essence of every ingredient

Soups are essential to every Chinese meal and they are so much a part of family life that in olden times, the first duty of a bride was to enter the kitchen on the third day of her marriage to prepare soup for her new family. Even today, in traditional households, the menu for lunch or dinner would comprise 'three dishes and a soup' or 'four dishes and a soup'. This custom is also followed by waiters in most Chinese restaurants when they make recommendations for a meal.

Soups are delicious, nutritious and easy to prepare. One need only put meat or vegetables in a pot of water and simmer it to make a tasty soup.

The Chinese put the idea across graphically in their writing. The character for simmer 煲 is literally to place the pot 保 over the fire 火. However, 保 could also mean 'to protect', a pun which conveys the idea that the pot also retains the nutrients in the ingredients. This is why left-over soups can be gently reheated without losing flavour or food value.

The fact that these natural flavours are highly valued by the Chinese means that little or no extra flavouring is added to their soups. The essence of each ingredient is coaxed out by the process of simmering. However, it is not only the expensive ingredients like snow fungus or shark's fin that are used, even the humble peanut or mundane pork ribs make wonderful soups.

The nature of the food determines which of the two simmering methods are used. Slice or shredded vegetables and chopped or minced meat are cooked by fast simmering 快滾. In this process, ingredients are added to boiling water and left to simmer for just about ten minutes before serving. A good example is Chinese Spinach Soup (see pg 127).

In slow simmering 慢滾, chunky pieces of meat and marrows are put into boiling water and left to simmer slowly for 3 to 4 hours. Pork and Lotus Root Soup (see pg 123) is an example.

In China, different soups are made during the different seasons of the year. Rejuvenating soups are prepared in springtime, refreshing soups are made for hot summer days, soups during the dry autumn months are designed to provide the system with much needed fluids, while fortifying soups are brewed for cold winter nights. These soups fall under one of the following six categories found in Chinese cuisine.

CLEAR SOUP 清汤 is the most common of Chinese soups. Like the Chinese White Cabbage Soup (see pg 136), they often contain vegetables and meat.

THICKENED SOUPS 羹 are thickened by the addition of cornflour. A well-known example is Shark's Fin and Crab Meat Soup (see pg 142).

SWEET CLEAR PASTES 露 are also thickened with cornflour, but in addition, beaten egg white is stirred in to produce what is known as the 'snow flake or dew effect'. Indeed, the character 露 is also the word for 'dew', which represents drops of rain 雨 on the road 路. Water Chestnut Paste (see pg 150) is a fine example of a soup cooked by this method.

SWEET PUREES 糊, of which Peanut Cream (see pg 143) is an example, require additional starchy thickening which may be a thicker cornflour solution, a cream or the liquid obtained by soaking uncooked rice in water.

SWEET BEAN SOUPS 沙 – (literally sand), usually made of beans that are cooked until the ingredients have broken down into sandy granules. A popular soup of this type is Sweet Red Bean Soup (see pg 145).

SWEET TEAS 茶, containing nuts and dried fruits, are traditionally brewed during auspicious occasions and served in ornate teacups to welcome guests. A popular sweet tea is Longan Tea (see pg 150).

SWEET SOUPS 糖水, – (literally sugared water), combine vegetables, sweet dried ingredients and rock sugar to make 'cooling' drinks for hot, dry spells. Six-Flavoured Sweet Soup (see page 144) is a good example.

To make a good soup, all meat and bones used must be cleaned and scalded to remove unwanted fat and smells. This will also minimise scum in the stock. Measure the amount of water required and use a large enough pot so that the water fills no more than 80 percent of the pot's capacity. This will ensure that the soup will not boil over when all the ingredients are put in.

Bring the water to a boil before adding any ingredients so that the ingredients will not be broken up by the boiling process and turn the soup chalky. However, the liquid should be kept on the boil over high heat for 15 minutes after the ingredients have been added before being simmered over low heat for the remaining cooking time.

Check the level of the soup occasionally when it is simmering, but never add more water at this stage as it will dilute the flavour of the soup. This is why it is important that sufficient water is used at the start and that the correct heat is used for cooking. Seasoning, if any, should be added to the soup only when it is done.

Skim the surface of the soup before serving. Excess oil skimmed from soups was once favoured as a glaze for the cooked food from the soup.

KITCHENWARE

Large claypot
Large saucepan
Pressure cooker
Crock pot
Ladle
Colander ladle
Colander

INGREDIENTS SUITABLE FOR SIMMERING

SEAFOOD	VEGETABLES	MISCELLANEOUS	MEAT
Fish with coarse flesh	Hairy marrow	Snow fungus	Lean pork
Fish bones	Old cucumber	Snow frog's gland	Pork rib
Abalone	Chinese cabbage	Dried abalone	Chicken
Sea cucumber	Watercress	Bean	Duck
Dried scallop	Bittergourd		Pigeon
Dried oyster	Sweet potato		

TEMPERATURE AND COOKING TIMES

Claypots and saucepans: 15 minutes at high heat, then simmer at medium to low heat for 3 to 4 hours.

Pressure cookers: After the whistle, cook for one-third of the time required in the recipe.

Crock Pot: Switch on to high and simmer for twice the time required for cooking over a gas stove.

節瓜湯

HAIRY MARROW SOUP

2 hairy marrows
200 g (7 oz) pork ribs
100 g (3.5 oz) lean pork
6 red dates, stoned
2 slices old ginger
20 g (0.7 oz) dried scallops
2.3 litres (9 cups) water

SEASONING
1 teaspoon salt
½ teaspoon light soya sauce

Wash and skin marrows. Cut each marrow crosswise into 5 pieces.

Wash and scald meat in hot water for 3 minutes.

Rinse and drain scallops.

Bring 2.3 litres (9 cups) of water to a boil. Add all the ingredients and boil over high flame for 15 minutes. Lower flame and simmer soup for 3 hours. Add seasoning before serving.

If you are looking for a soup for a child who has just recovered from an illness, this is it.

The Chinese consider hairy marrows 'neutral' vegetables and the soft, pulpy flesh is easily digestible after it is cooked.

This is also an 'everyday' soup recommended for the family all the year through.

PAPAYA, PEANUTS AND CHICKEN FEET SOUP

木瓜煲鷄脚

1 half-ripe papaya (appox. 1 kg, 2.2 lb)
100 g (3.5 oz) raw peanuts
10 chicken feet
300 g (10.5 oz) spare ribs
2 slices old ginger
2.3 litres (9 cups) water

SEASONING
1 teaspoon salt
1 tablespoon light soya sauce

Soak peanuts in water over night. Drain. Skin and halve papaya. Remove seeds, rinse and cut into big wedges. Rinse and drain peanuts. Wash chicken feet and cut off claws. Scald spare ribs in hot water for 3 minutes. Rinse.

Bring 2.3 litres (9 cups) of water to a boil. Add all the ingredients, cover pot and leave to boil for 15 minutes over high flame. Lower flame and simmer slowly for 3½ to 4 hours. Add seasoning.

Serve soup and cooked ingredients separately. Complement cooked ingredients with a little soya sauce.

There were papaya trees growing in the backyard of my childhood home, and they supplied the whole family with fruit all year round. Sometimes, instead of waiting for the fruit to fully ripen, my father would use half-ripened papayas in soups. These fruit, with only a hint of yellow, were plucked and left overnight for the sap to drain before being cooked.

Father believed that papayas fortify the lungs and he said chicken feet were used in this recipe to strengthen the legs.

四神湯 ☯

FOUR-HERB SOUP

20 g (0.7 oz) poria cocos (*fook lin*)
20 g (0.7 oz) euryale ferox (*see sat*)
20 g (0.7 oz) dioscorea (*wai san*)
20 g (0.7 oz) lotus seeds (*leen chee*)
200 g (7 oz) pork rib
200 g (7 oz) lean pork
2.3 litres (9 cups) water
1 teaspoon salt

Rinse herbs and lotus seeds briefly. Scald pork ribs and lean pork in hot water for 3 minutes.

Bring 2.3 litres (9 cups) of water to a boil. Add herbs, lotus seeds, pork ribs and lean meat. Boil for 15 minutes over high flame then lower flame and simmer slowly for 3½ hours. Season with 1 teaspoon salt if required.

Serve soup and ingredients separately. Complement with a little plate of soya sauce.

Fook Lin, botanically known as Poria Cocos, *is a white, chalky tuber-like root often found growing amongst the roots of pine trees in China.*

From ancient times, Chinese medical scholars have recorded that this herb has the effect of stimulating digestion and improving mental vitality.

魚
骨
湯
☯

FISH BONE SOUP

500g (1 lb) fish bones
100g (3.5 oz) soft beancurd
100g (3.5 oz) salted preserved mustard (*hum choy*)
1 carrot
3 slices old ginger
2 tablespoons oil
1 teaspoon salt, optional
1.9 litres (7½ cups) water

SALT SOLUTION FOR PRESERVED MUSTARD
625 ml (2½ cups) water
2 teaspoons salt

From childhood, the children of our family were often fed this soup.

My grandmother learnt from oral tradition that one must eat a lot of bony stuff to strengthen one's body structure. Her concept, of course, is equivalent to maintaining calcium intake for a balanced diet.

However, as children, we were not allowed to eat the fish bones. Grandmother told us that we had to drink "a lot of the soup as all the good things had gone inside the soup."

Wash fish bones well to remove scales and blood. Drain. Wash and drain beancurd. Wash, skin and cut carrot into big wedges.

Bring salt solution to a boil. Add the preserved mustard and boil for 10 minutes. Discard water, rinse and drain preserved mustard.

Bring 1.9 litres (7½ cups) of water to a boil. Meanwhile, heat 2 table-spoons of oil in a wok. When oil is smoking, add ginger and fry for 1 minute. Add fish bones and fry on both sides until light golden brown and fragrant.

Put all the ingredients and fried fish bones into the boiling water and leave to boil over high flame for 15 minutes. Lower flame and simmer soup for 2 hours. Add salt if necessary.

胡椒猪肚湯 ● PEPPER & PIG'S STOMACH SOUP

300 g (10.5 oz) spare ribs
1 pig's stomach
80 g (3 oz) white peppercorns
4 cloves garlic, crushed
4 teaspoons salt
2.3 litres (9 cups) water

SEASONING
1 teaspoon salt
1 tablespoon light soya sauce

Scald spare ribs in hot water for 3 minutes. Rinse.

Coat the inside of pig's stomach with 2 teaspoons salt and 2 cloves of crushed garlic thoroughly. Rinse. Repeat cleaning process again. Cook pig's stomach in 500 ml (2 cups) hot water for 5 minutes. Rinse.

Wash and drain peppercorns. Stuff pepper corns into pig's stomach. Seal opening with toothpicks.

Bring 2.3 litres (9 cups) of water to a boil. Add stuffed pig's stomach and boil over high flame for 15 minutes. Bring to a low falme and simmer for 3 hours. Season with 1 teaspoon of salt and 1 tablespoon light soya sauce if necessary.

Remove and discard peppercorns from stomach. Cut stomach into small slices and serve with a plate of light soya sauce. Serve soup hot.

This remarkable recipe is believed to have the effect of 'warming' the stomach to drive away 'wind'.

One Chinese food concept is that to strengthen part of one's body, one must eat the corresponding part of an animal's body. Here, to strengthen the stomach, pig's stomach is eaten while white pepper corns are added to relieve 'wind' from the body. You'll be surprised. It really works!

PORK & LOTUS ROOT SOUP

蓮藕瘦肉湯 ○

3 sections of lotus roots
100 g (3.5 oz) lean pork
200 g (7 oz) pork ribs
1 packet six-flavour ingredients (*lok mei*)
1 teaspoon salt
2.3 litres (9 cups) water

Scrub mud off lotus root and rinse well. Cut lotus root into sections near the joints to reveal the holes in the tuber.

Rinse lok mei ingredients briefly. Scald lean pork and pork ribs in hot water for 3 minutes.

Bring 2.3 litres (9 cups) of water to a boil. Add lotus root, pork and ribs and *lok mei* ingredients. Cover lid and boil over high flame for 30 minutes. Lower flame and simmer for 4 hours.

Season with salt. Slice lotus roots crosswise into 1 cm (½ in) sections, then serve soup and cooked ingredients with a little plate of light soya sauce.

"Hot weather always drains our energy quickly," that is what my mother used to say. So, to replenish lost energy, Mother made this soup for the family at least once a week during the hot season.

The crunchy lotus root and the six-flavour herb mixture make a rich, meaty soup said to strengthen the digestive system.

SNOW FUNGUS & GIZZARD SOUP

雪耳鴨腎湯 ☯

20 g (0.7 oz) snow fungus, soaked in warm water
2 preserved duck's gizzard, soaked in warm water
10 g (0.3 oz) sweet and bitter almond mixture (see page 213)
200 g (7 oz) lean pork
1 teaspoon salt
3 litres (12 cups) water

Soak snow fungus in warm water for 1 hour. Trim off stems and break fungus into florets. Drain. Wash and soak preserved duck's gizzard for 1 hour. Cut into thick slices. Rinse and drain almonds. Scald lean meat in hot water for 3 minutes. Rinse.

Bring 3 litres (12 cups) of water to a boil. Add all the ingredients and boil over high flame for 15 minutes. Lower flame and simmer for 3 hours. Season with salt if necessary.

Serve this soup hot and complement cooked ingredients with a little light soya sauce.

The distinctly salty flavour of pre-served duck's gizzards enhance the bland taste of the crunchy snow fungus in this recipe.

A very neutral soup believed to be soothing to the lungs, it is also said to alleviate 'heatiness'.

APPLE SOUP

蘋果湯 ☯

4 red apples
4 pieces crystallized Chinese figs (*mo fa kuo*)
150 g (5.5 oz) pork ribs
100 g (3.5 oz) lean pork
1.9 litres (7½ cups) water

SALT SOLUTION FOR APPLES
500 ml (2 cups) water
½ teaspoons salt

Wash and cut apples into halves. Remove the core but leave skin on. Soak apples in the salt solution for 1 minute. Drain.

Wash figs briefly and cut into halves.

Wash and scald meat in hot water for 3 minutes.

Bring 1.9 litres (7½ cups) of water to a boil. Add all the ingredients and cook over high flame for 15 minutes. Lower flame and simmer soup for 2½ hours. Season with ½ teaspoon salt. Serve with light soya sauce for dipping.

I am grateful to my two daughters' nanny who introduced me to this wonderful soup.

This apple and fig soup is a clear soup which is supposed to have the effect of soothing the lungs while fortifying brain power.

The figs used in this recipe are Chinese figs which are preserved by a glacing of sugar.

BITTERGOURD & DRIED OYSTERS SOUP

苦瓜蠔豉湯 ●

1 big bittergourd
300 g (10.5 oz) spare ribs
6 dried oysters, soaked in warm water
6 red dates, stoned
2 slices old ginger
1.9 litres (7½ cups) water
½ teaspoons salt

Soak dried oysters in warm water for 30 minutes and remove grit. Discard water. Cut bittergourd into big slices. Remove seeds. Scald spare ribs in hot water for 3 minutes.

Bring 1.9 litres (7½ cups) of water to a boil. Add all the ingredients, cover pot and leave to boil for 15 minutes over high heat. Lower heat and simmer slowly for 2½ hours.

Add ½ teaspoon salt if necessary. Serve soup separately from bittergourd and spare ribs. Serve hot.

My husband taught me this recipe after our marriage. He said that this soup is 'cooling' and said to benefit a person with frequent skin rashes.

When I first read the recipe, I wondered who would like this soup since bittergourds are bitter and I could not imagine drinking a bitter soup. However, the flavour of the dried oysters surpass the bitterness of the gourd and the soup, far from being bitter, has a special aftertaste.

CHINESE SPINACH SOUP

莧菜湯 ●

300 g (10.5 oz) Chinese spinach (*yeen choy*)
100 g (3.5 oz) minced pork
1 clove garlic, skinned and crushed
1 slice old ginger
1 tablespoon oil
1 teaspoon salt
1.1 litre (4½ cups) hot water

SEASONING
½ teaspoon salt
½ teaspoon sugar
½ teaspoon light soya sauce
1 teaspoon cornflour

Chinese spinach is a must in my family's diet. In fact I make sure that my children have this leafy vegetable at least once a week.

This spinach is high in iron and needs a little longer cooking time. You'll be surprised that this simple, refreshing soup can also alleviate constipation.

Pluck Chinese spinach into 8 cm (3 to 4 inch) lengths. Wash and drain.

Marinate minced pork with seasoning. Shape into small meatballs.

Heat 1 tablespoon of oil in a saucepan. When smoky put in garlic and ginger and sauté for 1 minute.

Add Chinese spinach and stir-fry for 2 to 3 minutes.

Pour in 1.1 litre (4½ cups) of hot water and bring it to a boil over high flame for 15 minutes. Lower flame and simmer soup for 10 minutes.

Add seasoned meat balls and simmer for another 10 minutes.

Season with 1 teaspoon of salt before serving.

赤小豆煲粉葛

KUDZU & GRAM BEAN SOUP

1 kudzu root *(fun kort)* (approx. 1 kg, 2.2 lb)
100 g (3.5 oz) gram beans *(chaik siew dao)*
2 slices old ginger
6 red dates, stoned
300 g (10.5 oz) spare ribs
100 g (3.5 oz) lean pork
2.3 litres (9 cups) water

SEASONING
1 teaspoon salt
1 tablespoon light soya sauce

Wash and skin kudzu. Cut into 2 cm (½ in) thick slices. Rinse gram beans and red dates briefly, then drain.

Scald spare ribs and lean pork in hot water for 3 minutes. Rinse.

Bring 2.3 litres (9 cups) of water to a boil. Add the ingredients. Bring to a boil again for 15 minutes and then lower flame and simmer soup for 3½ to 4 hours. Add seasoning.

Serve soup and cooked ingredients separately. Complement the cooked ingredients with light soya sauce.

Kudzu is the Japanese name for what the Cantonese call Fun Kort (literally, powdery bulb). It is a yam-like tuber that, when cooked, has a starchy yet fibrous texture. This seasonal vegetable is usually available around the Chinese New Year which falls in either January or February.

Maroon coloured gram beans are slightly longer than red beans and have a distinct white eye. They are said to be good for relieving water retention in the body and, when cooked with kudzu as in this recipe, results in a food reputed to cleanse the kidneys and bladder.

FROG & SEA MOSS SOUP

發菜田鷄湯 ●

500 g (1 lb) frog *(teen kai)*
20 g (0.7 oz) sea moss *(fatt choy), soaked*
10 Chinese mushrooms
2 slices old ginger
2.3 litres (9 cups) water

FOR SCALDING FROG AND SEA MOSS
2 slices old ginger
2 stalks spring onion
1 tablespoon Chinese rice wine
1.5 litres (6 cups) water

MARINADE
½ tablespoon ginger juice
1 teaspoon salt

SEASONING
1 teaspoon salt
½ teaspoon light soya sauce

We do not use patent laxatives in our family. Whenever constipation strikes, my mother would bring out the frogs and the sea moss!

This simple soup is very mild, yet delicious. It is believed to cleanse the major internal organs of the body, especially the large intestines.

Clean and soak mushrooms in 250 ml (1 cup) water for 15 minutes. Squeeze off excess water. Retain mushroom water for stock.
Soak sea moss for 15 minutes. Drain and discard water.

Skin and gut frog. Wash thoroughly and cut into serving pieces. Marinate for 10 minutes.

Bring scalding mixture to a boil. Put in marinated frog parts for 3 minutes. Ladle frog parts out and drain.

Put soaked sea moss into the same scalding mixture for 3 minutes. Drain. Discard scalding mixture.

Add the mushroom water to the remaining 2 litres (8 cups) water and bring to a boil. Add frogs, mushroom, sea moss and old ginger slices. Boil for 15 minutes and lower flame. Simmer soup for 1 hour. Add seasoning.

Serve soup and cooked ingredients separately.

NOTE: *Prepared frog parts are available in supermarkets in Singapore.*

眉豆冬菇腳湯 ●

BROW BEAN
& MUSHROOM STEM SOUP

50 g (2 oz) Chinese mushroom stems
8 red dates, stoned
100g (3.5 oz) brow beans (mei dao)
200 g (7 oz) lean spare ribs
100 g (3.5 oz) lean pork
1 piece preserved tangerine peel
2.3 litres (9 cups) water
Salt and light soya sauce to taste

Every time you trim the stems from Chinese mushrooms, save them for this recipe. You'll love the tasty soup which is said to stimulate the appetite. Brow beans are 'cooling' and this is thus a good soup to serve during the hot season.

Wash and soak brow beans for 1 hour. Wash and soak mushroom stems also for 1 hour. Trim stem ends. Rinse red dates and tangerine peel briefly and drain. Scald spare ribs and lean pork in hot water for 3 minutes. Rinse.

Bring 2.3 litres (9 cups) of water to a boil. Add ingredients and boil for 15 minutes. Lower flame and simmer soup for 3 hours. Season with salt and light soya sauce to taste.

Serve soup hot and complement cooked ingredients with a small plate of light soya sauce.

蓮子雞蛋糖水

LOTUS SEED & EGG SOUP

40 g (1.3 oz) lilium brownii (pak hup), rinsed
80 g (3 oz) lotus seeds
80 g (3 oz) rock sugar
4 hardboiled eggs, shelled
1.9 litres (7½ cups) water

The Chinese have a saying: What is good to the mouth must be good for the stomach, and what is good for the stomach must also be good for the mind.

Lotus seeds have all these assets. They have a sweet, mildly nutty taste and melt-in-the-mouth texture. They are believed to strengthen the stomach and the spleen, and are also said to have the effect of promoting sleep and memory. It is an ancient Chinese custom to serve this delicious snack on auspicious days to signify a fruitful event.

Bring 1.5 litres (6 cups) of water to a boil. Put in lotus seeds and continue to boil for 30 minutes over medium flame. Drain and rinse lotus seeds under cold running water. Rub skin off and soak lotus seeds in cold water. Drain before use.

Bring another 1.9 litres (7½ cups) of water to a boil. Add boiled lotus seeds, cover pot and boil for 15 minutes over high flame. Lower flame and simmer soup for 2 hours.

Add lilium brownii and rock sugar, and continue to simmer for 1 hour. Put in shelled eggs 15 minutes before serving. Serve hot.

鷄膶豆苗湯 PEA SHOOT & CHICKEN LIVER SOUP

2 chicken livers
100 g (3.5 oz) pea shoots (*dao miew*)
1 egg, beaten
2 slices old ginger
1 clove garlic, sliced
1.1 litres (4½ cups) hot water
1 teaspoon salt
1 tablespoon oil

MARINADE
1 teaspoon salt
½ teaspoon sugar
½ teaspoon light soya sauce
1 teaspoon oil

Pea shoots are the young, tender shoots of the snow pea vine. As such, it is a relatively expensive vegetable.

But who cares about price when research reveals that pea shoots should have the effects of increasing vitality and improving the complexion. Beaten egg and chicken livers are added to the recipe, to enhance the beautifying effect of this soup.

Wash and drain pea shoots.

Remove fat from chicken liver. Clean and rub thoroughly with 1 teaspoon salt, then rinse and drain. Chop finely and marinate.

Heat 1 tablespoon of oil in saucepan. When smoky, fry ginger and garlic till fragrant. Add marinated chicken liver and fry for another 2 minutes. Put in pea shoots and stir-fry for 1 minute. Add 1 teaspoon salt.

Pour in 1.1 litres (4½ cups) of hot water and bring to a boil. Boil for 2 minutes then turn off heat and remove pot from stove. Add in beaten egg slowly and stir well. Serve immediately.

白果冬瓜湯 ●

WINTER MELON & GINGKO NUTS SOUP

As early as the Tang Dynasty (618–907 AD), the Chinese were already aware of the properties of the winter melon. By the Sung Dynasty (960–1279 AD), scholars were recording that the melon had medicinal value.

Winter melon is a summer vegetable and is best served as a soup to 'quench thirst'. It is also reputed to be able to alleviate 'heatiness'. With the addition of gingko nuts in this recipe, the soup is said to be effective for relieving water retention in the body.

1 small winter melon (tung kwa), about 1 kg or 2.2 lb
30 g (1 oz) barley
3 slices old ginger
100 g (3.5 oz) gingko nuts
300 g (10.5 oz) pork ribs
1.9 litres (7½ cups) water

SEASONING
1 teaspoon salt
1 teaspoon light soya sauce

Skin and remove core and seeds from winter melon. Cut into 5 cm (2 inch) wedges. Wash and drain.

Rinse and drain barley. Shell gingko nuts and remove membrane. Rinse and drain. Scald spare ribs in hot water for 3 minutes. Rinse.

Bring 1.9 litres (7½ cups) of water to a boil. Add all the ingredients and boil for 15 minutes. Lower flame and simmer soup for 2 hours.

Add seasoning before serving.

珍珠豆湯

PEARLY BEAN SOUP

Pearly beans are large white beans about 1 cm (0.5 inch) in diameter. Four or five beans grow inside beautifully dappled rose-red and white bean pods measuring about 10 cm (4 inches) long. The beans resemble big, round pearls, hence the name pearly beans. Pearly beans are available at wet markets all year round.

It was my post-natal amah who taught me this recipe. She said that this soup has the effect of alleviating 'dampness' from the body.

500 g (1 lb) pearly beans in pods (chun chue dao)
200 g (7 oz) pork ribs
2 slices old ginger
2.3 litres (9 cups) water
1 teaspoon salt

Separate beans from pods. Wash beans and drain. Scald pork ribs in hot water for 3 minutes.

Bring 2.3 litres (9 cups) of water to the boil. Add all the ingredients, cover pot and leave to boil for 15 minutes over high heat. Lower heat and simmer slowly for 2 hours. Season with 1 teaspoon salt if necessary.

Serve soup and ingredients separately. Provide a little plate of soya sauce for the beans. This soup must be served hot.

芥菜燒鴨湯 ●

LEAF MUSTARD WITH ROAST DUCK SOUP

500 g (1.1 lb) leaf mustard (*kai choy*)
Half a roast duck
2 slices old ginger
1 tablespoon oil
1.9 litres (7½ cups) hot water
1 teaspoon salt

Whenever we have a hearty meal of roasted duck for dinner, we often save the leftovers for making this soup the next day.

Leaf mustard has a bitter aftertaste when cooked, but the Chinese consider that whatever tastes bitter has a 'cooling' effect on the body. This soup is, therefore, reputed to be good for alleviating 'heatiness'.

Wash and drain leaf mustard, then cut into 3 sections (about 8 cm or 3 inch). Cut roasted duck into serving pieces.

Heat pot with 1 tablespoon oil and when smoky, add in ginger slices and fry for 30 seconds. Stir in the leaf mustard and fry for 2 minutes. Add in the roasted duck and mix well.

Pour in 1.9 litres (7½ cups) of hot water and boil for 10 minutes. Lower heat and simmer soup for 30 minutes. Add 1 teaspoon of salt or to taste. Serve soup seperately from leaf mustard and roasted duck. Serve hot.

白菜湯 ●

CHINESE WHITE CABBAGE SOUP

5 heads Chinese white cabbage (*pak choy*)
200 g (7 oz) spare ribs
100 g (3.5 oz) lean pork
8 red dates, stoned
1 piece preserved tangerine peel
2 slices old ginger
1.9 litres (7½ cups) water

SEASONING
½ teaspoon salt
½ teaspoon soya sauce

This is one of my favourite soups for the hot season.

However, though a favourite it may be, I do not serve it too often because Chinese white cabbage is considered by traditionalists to be highly 'cooling'. That is why a piece of preserved tangerine peel is added to the soup to neutralise some of the 'yin' essence.

Wash cabbages. Cut each stalk into 3 sections. Scald spare ribs and lean pork in hot water for 3 minutes. Rinse tangerine peel and red dates.

Bring 1.9 litres (7½ cups) of water to a boil.

Add all the ingredients, cover pot and leave to boil for 15 minutes over high heat. Lower heat and simmer slowly for 3 hours. Add seasoning.

Serve soup and ingredients seperately. Serve hot.

蕃薯糖水 ☯

SWEET POTATO SOUP

400 g (14 oz) sweet potatoes
1 sprig pandanus leaves
2 slices old ginger
10 g (0.3 oz) dried longan flesh, optional
100 g rock sugar
1.9 litres (7½ cups) water

Clean and skin sweet potatoes. Cut sweet potatoes into 3 cm (1½ inch) cubes. Wash pandanus leaf and knot it. Rinse rock sugar and dried longan flesh before use.

Bring 1.9 litres (7½ cups) of water to a boil. Add sweet potatoes, pandanus leaf, ginger and dried longan flesh and boil for 15 minutes over high flame. Lower flame and leave soup to simmer for 1 hour.

Add the rock sugar and continue to simmer soup for another 30 minutes. Remove pandanus leaf and ginger before serving. Serve warm.

Do not think that just because sweet potatoes are cheap, they have no food value. In fact, sweet potatoes are very nutritious and are an especially suitable food for invalids since, once cooked, they are soft and easily digestible.

There are several varieties of this tuber that have different coloured flesh: creamy beige, orange, and purple. I prefer the purple-fleshed variety as I have been told that is is very high in protein and minerals.

Pandanus leaves and longan flesh are combined here with sweet potato to make a nourishing light snack which I highly recommend for the hot season.

老黄瓜煲羅漢果 ●

OLD CUCUMBER WITH BUDDHA'S FRUIT

1 large old cucumber
½ Buddha's fruit *(lo hon kuo)*
2.3 litres (9 cups) water

Wash and quarter old cucumber. Discard pith and seeds. Rinse Buddha's fruit.

Bring 2.3 litres (9 cups) of water to a boil. Add old cucumber and Buddha's fruit, cover pot and boil for 15 minutes over high flame. Lower flame and simmer soup for 2 hours.

When soup is done, let it cool and serve it warm.

This is a refreshing sweet drink for a hot day as it is supposed to soothe dry lungs.

Buddha's fruit is dark brown, round and surprisingly light in weight. It has a sharp, sweet taste. The name is derived from the fact that the fruit grows in clusters of eighteen, exactly the number of Buddha's close disciples. The fruit, grown in China's Kwangsi province, is easily available from all Chinese medical shops.

栗子鷄湯 ○

Every year, around October, I look forward to the arrival of fresh chestnuts which are not only delicious but nutritious. The Chinese believe that chestnuts strengthen the spleen, stomach and kidneys. I remember the old man who used to push his cart around our neighbourhood in Chinatown, selling chestnuts fried to a deep, golden brown. He fried batches in a mixture of pebbles and sugar for an hour or more until the fragrance drew us to his stall.

As much as I loved chestnuts fried in this way, my nanny forbade me to have too many in case I developed a sore throat. Fortunately, she allowed me to have as many as I wanted when they were cooked in soup. This is Nanny's recipe.

CHESTNUT & CHICKEN SOUP

1 medium chicken (1.5 kg, 3.3 lb)
1 kg (2.2 lb) fresh chestnuts
1 teaspoon salt, or to taste
6 litres (24 cups) water

Clean and gut chicken. Scald in hot water for 3 minutes. Rinse. Bring 3 litres (12 cups) water to a boil. Add in chestnuts and boil for 15 minutes. Discard water and rinse chestnuts. Shell chestnuts and remove membranes with a small knife.

Bring another 3 litres (12 cups) of water to a boil. Add in all the ingredients. Cover pot and leave to boil for 15 minutes over high heat. Lower heat and simmer slowly for 2 hours. Add salt to taste.

Serve soup and ingredients separately. Provide light soy sauce to complement cooked ingredients. Serve hot.

蓮藕鱆魚湯

Lotus root is the tuber of a species of water lily. In wet markets, the roots are offered for sale still covered with a coat of mud from the lily pond. This sticky, grey covering, it seems, helps keep the root fresh.

I love the sweet, mild flavour of the variety of lotus root which has a crunchy bite. My grandmother, however, preferred the type with a starchy texture which is considered a better grade.

The Chinese believe that lotus root can purify blood and dried octopus has the effect of improving blood circulation.

DRIED OCTOPUS & LOTUS ROOT SOUP

1 lotus root with 3 or 4 sections
500 g (1 lb) lean pork
2 slices old ginger
8 red dates, stoned
10 g (0.3 oz) dried octopus
1 teaspoon salt
3 litres (12 cups) water

Scrub mud off lotus root and rinse well. Cut the root into sections near the joints to reveal the holes in the tuber.

Scald lean pork in hot water for 3 minutes. Wash dried octopus and cut into big slices. Rinse and drain red dates.

Bring 3 litres (12 cups) of water to a boil. Add all the ingredients, cover pot and leave to boil for 15 minutes over high heat. Lower heat and simmer slowly for 4 hours, then season with 1 teaspoon of salt.

Slice lotus root crosswise into 1 cm (½ inch) sections, then serve soup and ingredients separately. Provide light soya sauce to complement cooked ingredients. Serve hot.

絲瓜魚片湯 ●

ANGLED LUFFA FISH SLICE SOUP

1 angled luffa (*see kwa*) about 400 g, 14 oz
200 g (7 oz) white fish fillet
100 g (3.5 oz) lean pork, sliced
50 g (1.75 oz) carrot, skinned and sliced
10 g (0.3 oz) button mushrooms, sliced
2 slices old ginger
1 tablespoon oil
1 egg, lightly beaten
1.1 litres (4½ cups) hot water
1 teaspoon salt

MARINADE FOR FISH
½ teaspoon salt
½ teaspoon light soy sauce
1 tablespoon oil
Dash of pepper

MARINADE FOR LEAN PORK
½ teaspoon salt
½ teaspoon light soy sauce
½ teaspoon oil

My grandmother had always referred to those who deceived her as 'angled luffas' 丝瓜. She explained that this is because under the tough, ridged and dark green skin of the gourd is a white spongy flesh – very deceptive in appearance indeed.

My husband enjoys this refreshing soup which is ideal for the hot season since angled luffas possess 'cooling' qualities.

Peel angled luffa and cut into wedges. Slice fish and lean pork thinly and marinade for ten minutes in respective marinades. Wash and slice carrot and button mushrooms. Drain.

Heat saucepan with 1 tablespoon oil. When smoky, add in ginger and fry till fragrant.

Add in carrot and mushrooms. Fry for 2 minutes. Add in angled luffa and fry for 1 minute. Now, pour in 1.1 litres (4½ cups) hot water and bring mixture to a boil.

Include lean pork and boil over medium heat for 5 minutes. Add in fish slices and season with 1 teaspoon salt. Turn off heat and remove pot from stove.

Add in beaten egg slowly and stir well. Serve immediately.

蟹黃魚翅

SHARK'S FIN & CRAB MEAT SOUP

200 g (7 oz) pre-soaked shark's fin
50 g (2 oz) steamed crab meat
1 egg, beaten

SEASONING
1 teaspoon salt
1 teaspoon light soya sauce
½ teaspoon dark soya sauce
1 tablespoon oil
Dash of pepper

STOCK
200 g (7 oz) chicken bones
100 g (3.5 oz) pork ribs
1 dried scallop, rinsed
2.3 litres (9 cups) water

SCALDING SOLUTION
2 slices old ginger
2 stalks spring onion
1 teaspoon Chinese rice wine
1.5 litres (6 cups) water

CORNFLOUR THICKENING
2 tablespoons cornflour
2 tablespoons water

To make a perfect shark's fin and crab meat soup, you must use a rich base as shark's fin, in itself, is very bland. I would advise that you use freshly steamed crab meat in this recipe for that distinctive seafood taste. The timing for the addition of the beaten egg is also very important since the ribbons of egg must be cooked yet maintain a light, smooth texture.

Lastly, complement the soup with Chinese red vinegar, prefarably from Chekiang.

Prepare stock by simmering ingredients for 1 hour until it is reduced to 1.1 litres (4½ cups). Sieve stock through muslin cloth.

Bring scalding solution to a boil and add in the soaked shark's fin. Simmer over medium heat for 15 minutes. Drain and rinse shark's fin. Discard solution, including spring onions and ginger.

Heat a wok. Put in stock and shark's fin and bring to a boil. Include seasoning and crab meat. Stir well.

Thicken with cornflour mixture and stir briskly for 2 minutes. Switch off heat. Slowly stir in beaten egg.

Serve shark's fin soup hot in a tureen. Complement with a little plate of red Chinese vinegar.

PEANUT CREAM

花生糊

200 g (7 oz) raw peanuts
150 g (5.5 oz) raw rice
150 g (5.5 oz) rock sugar
125 ml (½ cup) fresh milk
1.1 litres (4½ cups) oil
2.3 litres (9 cups) water

CORNFLOUR THICKENING
4 tablespoons cornflour
4 tablespoons water

Rinse rice briefly and drain. Put the rice in a wok and fry without oil for about 5 minutes over very low flame until light golden brown. Cool and rinse, then drain thoroughly.

Heat 1.1 litres (4½ cups) oil in a wok and, when hot, add in raw peanuts and deep-fry for 5 minutes. Drain and cool.

Put rice and peanuts in 2.3 litres (9 cups) water. Grind or use blender to mash up contents until it is chalky, then use a muslin cloth to sieve the contents. Discard the dregs.

Pour blended peanut and rice into a saucepan over medium heat and keep stirring all the time until the contents boil.

Add in rock sugar and continue to cook for another 15 minutes. Thicken with cornflour mixture and keep stirring for 2 minutes. Switch off heat. Stir in the fresh milk and serve hot.

The Chinese have always believed that the body needs some form of oil to soothe it and assist its function. The natural vegetable oils coaxed out of peanuts through the process of simmering is favoured for this purpose.

My grandmother used to cook this tempting snack for us. She told me that this peanut cream can improve my complexion and that it can also strengthen our nails and hair.

六味湯 ☯

SIX-FLAVOURED SAVOURY SOUP

10 g (0.3 oz) dried longan flesh
10 g (0.3 oz) dioscorea (*wai san*)
10 g (0.3 oz) lilium brownii (pak hup)
10 g (0.3 oz) euryale ferox (*see sut*)
20 g (0.75 oz) polyconattum (*yok chok*)
20 g (0.75 oz) lotus seeds (*leen chee*)
200 g (7 oz) spare ribs
100 g (3.5 oz) lean pork
2.3 litres (9 cups) water
1 teaspoon salt

This recipe is an excellent example of a light Chinese tonic. Lok is Cantonese for 'six' and Mei means 'flavours', so Lok Mei is a herbal mixture of six fragrant herbs.

Do not worry yourself over the names of the individual herbs contained in the mix, but simply go to a Chinese herbal shop and ask for Lok Mei and you will not go wrong.

The various flavours of the herbs combine well to make a delicious soup with a sweet, meaty taste. It is said to be good for stimulating appetite and restoring general health.

Rinse all herbs, dried longan flesh and lotus seeds. Scald meat in hot water for 3 minutes. Rinse. Bring 2.3 litres (9 cups) of water to a boil. Then add rinsed ingredients and the meat.

Cover pot and leave to boil for 15 minutes over high heat. Lower flame and simmer slowly for 3½ hours. The soup is ready when the dioscorea becomes translucent.

Season with 1 teaspoon of salt, and serve soup and ingredients separately. Complement with a little plate of light soya sauce.

六味糖水 ☯

SIX-FLAVOURED SWEET SOUP

10g (0.3 oz) dried longan flesh
10g (0.3 oz) dioscorea (*wai san*)
10g (0.3 oz) lilium brownii (pak hup)
10g (0.3 oz) euryale ferox (*see sut*)
20g (0.75 oz) polyconattum (*yok chok*)
20g (0.75 oz) lotus seeds (*leen chee*)
100g (3.5 oz) rock sugar
2.3 litres (9 cups) water

If you are looking for a change from meaty soups which are so much a part of a healthy Chinese diet, this recipe is the end of your search.

The six-flavoured ingredients, beside being used for cooking savoury soups, is also the basis for this refreshing sweet snack which is reputed to be good for general health.

Best consumed during hot, dry weather, this sweet soup and the cooked ingredients can be served hot or chilled.

Rinse herbs and lotus seeds.

Bring 2.3 litres (9 cups) of water to a boil. Add cleaned herbs and lotus seeds, cover pot and leave to boil for 15 minutes over high heat. Lower heat and simmer slowly for 2 hours.

Add the rock sugar and continue to simmer for 1 hour. The soup is ready when the dioscorea become translucent. Serve hot or chilled.

MUNG BEAN CONGEE

綠豆水 ●

50 g (2 oz) mung or green beans (luk dao)
30 g (1 oz) rice
100 g (3.5 oz) rock sugar, rinsed
1 small piece preserved tangerine peel, rinsed
2 litres (8 cups) hot water

Wash mung beans and rice together. Drain, and put mixture together with tangerine peel into a saucepan. Add 2 litres (8 cups) of hot water. Cover lid and leave to boil for 15 minutes over high heat. Lower heat and simmer slowly for 2 hours. Check water level occasionally.

Put in rock sugar and continue to cook on low heat for 1 hour.

FOR CROCK-POT USERS: *Use 1.3 litres (5 cups) of water and cook at high heat for 4 hours then add rock sugar and continue to cook for another 2 hours.*

I was given this sweet soup whenever my mother saw pimples appearing on my face. She told me that this soup would get rid of the 'heatiness' which invited pimples.

Sure enough, it worked! Not only did my pimples subside, but I also felt refreshed after having a couple of bowls.

SWEET RED BEAN SOUP

紅豆沙 ○

100 g (3.5 oz) red beans
50 g (2 oz) lotus seeds
2 small pieces dried tangerine peel, about 5g
120 g (4.2 oz) rock sugar
3.1 litres (12½ cups) water

Bring 1.3 litres (5 cups) water to a boil. Put in the lotus seeds and boil over medium heat for 30 minutes. Rinse lotus seeds under cold running water. Rub off skin and soak lotus seeds in cold water. Drain before use.

Wash red beans briefly and drain. Rinse tangerine peel briefly.

Bring 1.9 litres (7½ cups) water to a boil. Put in the red beans, lotus seeds and tangerine peel. Boil over high heat for 15 minutes. Lower heat and simmer for 2 hours (by this time the red beans and lotus seeds should be soft). Also check liquid level.

Add rock sugar and continue to simmer for 30 minutes. Serve hot or chilled.

Dried tangerine peel is one of the three treasures of the Cantonese. My ancestral village of Sun Wui 新会 in Kwantung province produces the best grade of tangerine peel. In general, the longer the aging process of the peel, the better the quality will be.

Whenever my grandmother cooked this soup, she would see to it that a piece of dried tangerine peel is added. She stored her tangerine peel in an air-tight biscuit tin which she hid under her bed. So you can see how precious tangerine peel can be!

On the fifth day of the Fifth Moon (the Dragon Boat Festival), we children would be bathed in a tubful of water strewn with fragrant flowers. Then, nicely dressed and smelling so sweet, we would have boiled glutinous rice dumplings and this sweet porridge for lunch.

My maternal grandmother told me that this porridge would drive all evil elements from our bodies. What she meant was that the beans used in this recipe are believed to release 'dampness' from the system.

SWEET FIVE-BEAN CONGEE

20 g (0.7 oz) red beans (*hong dao*)
20 g (0.7 oz) mung or green beans (*luk dao*)
20 g (0.7 oz) brow beans (*mei dao*)
20 g (0.7 oz) soya beans (*wong dao*)
20 g (0.7 oz) gram beans (*chaik siew dao*)
20 g (0.7 oz) rice
100 g rock sugar
1.1 litres (7½ cups) water

Wash the beans and rice briefly. Drain.

Bring the 1.1 litres (7½ cups) of water to a boil. Add the beans and rice, cover pot and boil for 30 minutes over high flame. Lower flame and keep simmering until grains begin to break open (about 1½ hours).

Add in rock sugar and simmer for another 1 hour.

Check water level occasionally to see if congee has thickened sufficiently. Serve warm.

白果薏米水 ●

When our nannies discovered that we children had very yellowish urine, they would cook this sweet soup for us. They believed that gingko nuts, beancurd strips and barley have the effect of cleansing the bladder and kidneys.

Mind that you drink this soup in the day if you do not want to make too many trips to the bathroom in the dead of the night.

GINGKO NUT & BARLEY SOUP

80 g (3 oz) shelled gingko nuts
50 g (2 oz) barley
50 g (2 oz) dried beancurd strips
100 g (3.5 oz) rock sugar
1.1 litres (7½ cups) water

Rinse barley. Break beancurd strips into 5 cm (2 inch) sections and soak in water for 15 minutes. Drain. Rinse barley and rock sugar.

Bring 1.1 litres (7½ cups) of water to a boil. Add gingko nuts, barley and dried beancurd strips. Cover pot and boil for 15 minutes over high heat. Lower heat and simmer soup for 1 hour.

Add rock sugar and continue to simmer for 1 hour. When the soup is ready, the beancurd strips should be broken up and resemble cooked beaten eggs. Serve warm.

The Chinese have a name for water-cress which is steeped in history.

'The Vegetable from the Western Oceans' 西洋菜 is not native to China and the name reflects the fact that the vegetable was first introduced by Portuguese sailors via Macau more than a century ago.

Watercress appears in savoury and sweet dishes. This sweet soup, believed to be very refreshing and soothing for the lungs, is drunk during hot weather.

There are two varieties of water-cress. One with thicker stems are grown in dry soil, while the variety with thin stems, dark green leaves and tender shoots grow in shallow ponds. The latter type is the popular choice.

西洋菜煲蜜棗 ●

WATERCRESS & HONEY DATE SOUP

1 kg (2.2 lb) watercress
10 honey dates
1.1 litres (7½ cups) water

Trim off the roots of the watercress. Soak watercress in water and pluck off the little roots growing along the stems. Wash and drain watercress again.

Bring 1.1 litres (7½ cups) of water to a boil. Add watercress and honey dates, cover pot and keep boiling for 15 minutes over high heat. Lower heat and simmer for 2 hours. This soup can be served hot or cold.

魚翅煲鷄腳 ○

SHARK'S FIN & CHICKEN FEET SOUP

You may wonder why an expensive delicacy like shark's fin should be cooked with chicken feet. This is because chicken feet provides a gelatinous consistency to the soup and enhances the bland taste of the shark's fins.

I was a sprinter during my school-days and my father cooked this soup, saying it would be good for me. He assured me that this was one of the best recipes for improving the complexion and toning the muscles. Thanks to Father and his shark's fin chicken soup, I managed to possess both qualities.

400 g (14 oz) pre-soaked shark's fins
10 chicken feet
2 slices old ginger
1 piece preserved tangerine peel
1.1 litres (7½ cups) water

FOR SCALDING SHARK'S FIN
2 stalks spring onion
2 slices old ginger
1 tablespoon Chinese rice wine
1.3 litres (5 cups) water

SEASONING
1 teaspoon salt
1 teaspoon light soya sauce

Wash and drain shark's fin.

Bring scalding solution to a boil. Put in shark's fin and simmer for 10 minutes over medium flame. Drain. Discard solution, including spring onions and ginger.

Wash chicken feet and cut off the claws. Rinse tangerine peel briefly.

Bring 1.1 litres (7½ cups) of water to a boil. Put in chicken feet and simmer over low heat for 2 hours. Add shark's fin, ginger, tangerine peel and continue to cook for 1 hour. Season with salt and light soya sauce if necessary.

Serve soup hot. Complement chicken feet and shark's fin with a little plate of light soya sauce.

RED BEAN & CHICKEN FEET SOUP

紅豆煲鷄脚○

200 g (7 oz) red beans
100 g (3.5 oz) raw peanuts
1 piece dried tangerine peel
3 cloves garlic
10 chicken feet
2.3 litres (9 cups) water
1 teaspoon salt, or to taste

Each member of my family has a head of thick, black hair. This can be attributed to my grandmother's effort in cooking this soup for us.

The Chinese believe that beans and nuts contain oils that nourish the hair. One of my students even reported to me that her hair became so 'obedient' after just one serving of this soup!

Wash and soak peanuts overnight. Drain. Wash and drain beans. Rinse tangerine peel. Wash and crush garlic cloves lightly. Do not peel off skin. Clean chicken feet and trim off claws.

Bring 2.3 litres (9 cups) of water to a boil. Add all the ingredients, cover pot and leave to boil for 15 minutes over high heat. Lower heat and simmer slowly for 4 hours. Check water level occasionally; lower heat if soup is reduced too quickly. Season with 1 teaspoon salt if necessary.

Serve soup and cooked ingredients separately with a little light soya sauce.

YOK CHOK CHICKEN SOUP

玉竹煲鷄

200 g (7 oz) polygonattum (*yok chok*)
1 medium chicken (1.5 kg, 3.3 lb)
20 g (0.7 oz) medlar seeds (*kei chee*)
2.5 litres (10 cups) water
1 teaspoon salt, or to taste
1.3 litres (5 cups) hot water for scalding

Whenever my mother sees me applying expensive nourishing creams to my face, she would advise me to save money on cosmetics, and prepare this less costly soup instead. She said that yok chok has a soothing effect on the complexion and that medlar seeds add sparkle to the eyes.

Clean and gut chicken. Scald in 1.3 litres (5 cups) hot water for 3 minutes. Rinse. Wash herbs briefly.

Bring 2.5 litres (10 cups) water to a boil. Add in all the ingredients. Cover pot and leave to boil for 15 minutes over high heat. Lower heat and simmer slowly for 3 hours. Add salt to taste.

Serve soup and cooked ingredients separately. Provide light soy sauce to complement cooked ingredients.

龍
眼
茶
○

LONGAN TEA

20 g (0.75 oz) dried longan flesh
10 g (0.3 oz) rice
8 red dates, stoned
1 slice old ginger
30 g (1 oz) rock sugar
1.1 litres (4½ cups) water

It is customary for the Chinese to serve longan tea as a welcome drink to guests during auspicious days. This is because longans have long been looked upon as a fruit of 'sweetness and roundness', which in Chinese minds mean 'everything will be perfect.'

Older folk favour this recipe which includes pan-fried rice. They believe that adding the rice would help in the 'warming of the stomach'. What they mean is that this drink is both appetising and an appetiser.

Wash rice and drain. Fry in wok (without oil) over very low flame for about 5 minutes until rice turns golden brown. Cool.

Rinse dried longan flesh and remove grit. Rinse red dates and rock sugar.

Bring 1.1 litres (4½ cups) of water to a boil. Add rice grains, cleaned longan flesh, stoned red dates and ginger. Cover pot and boil for 15 minutes over high flame.

Put in rock sugar, lower flame and simmer for 30 minutes. Serve hot.

馬
蹄
露
●

WATER CHESTNUT PASTE

10–12 water chestnuts
100 g (3.5 oz) rock sugar
1 egg
4 tablespoons cornflour
1.3 litres (5 cups) water

I just could not resist this sweet paste whenever my father prepared it as a chilled dessert for his restaurant during the hot season.

It is a very simple recipe, but the result is believed to be good for relieving internal heat and for soothing the digestive tract.

Wash and skin water chestnuts. Dice or mash finely.

Bring 1.3 litres (5 cups) of water to a boil. Add rock sugar and water chestnuts, and keep boiling for 15 minutes. Lower flame and simmer for 15 minutes until soup begins to thicken.

Mix the cornflour with 8 tablespoons water and use this mixture to thicken the soup. Remove pot from stove.

Beat egg in a bowl. Stir the beaten egg into the soup just before serving. Serve hot or chilled.

STEWING

Stew to create tender. flavourful and easily digestable food.

Stewing, the process of cooking by slowly simmering ingredients in a little liquid until all the ingredients are tender, is a basic method of Chinese cooking.

The Chinese character for stewing 焖 has three parts. The ideogram for fire 火 appears on the left while on the right, the word for heart or essence 心 appears locked behind a door 门. Put together, the ideograms show that by the process of stewing, the ingredients are not only made tender but that the essence of the food is drawn out and retained in the dish, thus presenting the true taste of the food.

Stewing is a popular method because stews can be prepared in advance and generally left unattended till the gravy is thickened just before serving. This thickening not only creates a rich, creamy sauce that can be eaten with rice, but also gives body to the tender and easily digestible food. Another advantage which makes stews a cook's favourite is that a stewed dish can be kept for nearly a week, its flavour improving with each reheating.

A few basic and important points must be followed when preparing a stew. Firstly, the flavours and textures of the ingredients must be carefully noted and selected to complement each other.

Second, woven bamboo sheets should be placed at the bottom of the pot to prevent the ingredients from sticking to the pot during the long cooking time.

Third, medium to low heat is generally used as high heat will cause meat to break into pieces instead of being tenderised.

Fourth, to keep vegetables crispy, soft vegetables should be put into the stew only a few minutes before serving. Hard vegetables, on the other hand, are usually parboiled separately and put into the stew an hour after cooking begins.

Fifth, all the ingredients must be covered with liquid when stewing begins so that the flavours will be evenly spread. The seasoning should also be carefully checked before thickening the gravy.

Sixth, one must master the control of heat during stewing because of the long cooking time required. Also, check the liquid level occasionally. In some stewing methods, the gravy 汁 is poured out and then cooked briskly with thickening for a minute or two to make a sauce 献, literally, 'to present'. This is poured over the stewed ingredients just before serving. This method is used in Braised Comb Shark's Fins (see pg 188).

Besides the basic slow stewing method, the Chinese have variations of this technique. They are fast stewing, braising, spicy stewing and sautéed stewing.

SLOW STEWING 焖

For this method, the ingredients are first steamed or deep fried. Liquid is then added and the dish is simmered over low heat for two hours till the ingredients become tender and succulent. Stewed Sea Cucumber and Duck (pg 167) is an example.

FAST STEWING 燴

Unlike the other methods of stewing, fast stewing, as the name implies, has a relatively shorter cooking time. A variety of ingredients are sliced and seasoned, and they are combined with a stock to simmer for 10 minutes. (The character 燴 indicates the use of fire 火 to bring ingredients together as 會 literally means 'to meet'.) This stock is then thickened with cornflour and the resulting gravy poured over previously prepared ingredients such as rice or, as in the case of Ma Por Tofu (pg 193), beancurds.

BRAISING 烧

An analysis of the character for braising will give a basis of this method. A combination of the ideogram for fire 火 and the word for sprinkle 尧, braising is to simmer the main ingredient in a little hot oil or water.

CLEAR BRAISING 熠 is to cook the main ingredient (usually meat or poultry) by simmering in water. No sauces are used and the meat is served with dipping sauces or condiments. Stewed Sweet Sour Pig's Trotter (pg 166) is a good example.

RED BRAISING 红烧 is used to cook larger cuts of meat and whole poultry. The meat is put into a highly heated saucepan with some oil and left to brown on all sides to seal in the juices. Seasonings are then added, especially light soya sauce for flavour and dark soya sauce for colour. Liquid is poured in to cover the meat and the mixture brought to a boil. Once the liquid begins to boil, the heat is reduced to very low, the pot is covered and the

dish is left to stew for two hours. The meat must be turned and the level of the liquid checked occasionally to ensure that the meat is evenly coated with the seasoning. Stewed Pork Loin (pg 200) is an example of a dish cooked by this method.

SPICY STEWING 滷

Used chiefly on offal, meat and poultry, this method of stewing cooks the ingredients in a spicy stock which is not served with the food. Instead, the stock is kept and used again. Vegetables are not cooked by this method as the juices from the vegetables will dilute and spoil the stock. An example of a dish prepared by this method is Stewed Spicy Chicken Giblets (pg 169).

SAUTÉED STEWING 熁

In sautéed stewing, spring onions, garlic and shallots are sautéed in a saucepan with heated oil until fragrant. Meat and a little liquid is then added to the oil and the mixture is stewed slowly until the meat is tender. An example of sautéed stewing is Stewed Carp with Spring Onion and Ginger (pg 187).

KITCHENWARE

Wok with cover
Claypot with lid
Saucepan with cover
Wok spatula
Soup ladle
Strainer
Weaved bamboo sheets

INGREDIENTS SUITABLE FOR STEWING

SEAFOOD	VEGETABLES	MISCELLANEOUS	MEAT
Sea cucumber	Chinese cabbage	Mushroom	Pork
Fish maw	Crystal lettuce	Straw mushroom	Beef
Dried mussel	Winter melon	Cloud fungus	Mutton
Dried abalone	Hairy marrow	Wood fungus	Chicken
Dried oyster	Bittegourd	Dried lily bud	Duck
Dried scallop	Broccoli	Sea moss	Pigeon
Carp	Spanish onion	Raw peanut	Frog
Fish head	Spring onion	Red date	Game
Turtle	Young ginger root	Beancurd	
Tortoise	Carrot	Dried pig tendon	
	Potato	Mungbean thread	
		Offal	

TEMPERATURE AND COOKING TIMES

METHOD	PREPARATION	COOKING	TEMPERATURE
Slow stewing	15 minutes	2 hours	Medium to low
Fast stewing	30 minutes	10 minutes	High heat
Braising	15 minutes	2 hours	Medium
Spicy stewing	15 minutes	2 hours	Medium
Sauteed stewing	15 minutes	30 minutes	High to low

焗
鷄
球
○

STEWED CHICKEN WITH GINGER AND ONIONS

½ medium-sized chicken (750 g, 1.5 lb)
8 slices old ginger
1 clove garlic, sliced
2 Spanish onions, wedged
2 stalks spring onions, cut into 5 cm (2 inch) lengths
1 big green pepper (capsicum), deseeded and wedged
1 small carrot, skinned and wedged
1 tablespoon oil
1.1 litres (4½ cups) oil
375 ml (1½ cups) water

MARINADE FOR CHICKEN
1 teaspoon salt
1 teaspoon sugar
1 teaspoon light soya sauce
1 teaspoon dark soya sauce
1 tablespoon Chinese rice wine
1 tablespoon oyster sauce
2 tablespoons cornflour
1 tablespoon oil

SEASONING
1 teaspoon salt
1 teaspoon sugar
½ teaspoon light soya sauce

When we were teenagers, Mother made it a point to check our complexion. If we were pale and slightly off-colour, she would pronounce that we had a lot of 'wind' in us!

Her remedy was to cook us something with old ginger since nothing eliminates 'wind' better than that.

This is no old-wives' tale and you will be surprised how much better you look, and how much more comfortable you feel, after all the 'wind' has been driven from your body.

Clean and wash chicken. Cut into serving pieces. Marinate for 30 minutes. Deep-fry in 1.1 litres (4½ cups) oil for 3 minutes to seal in juices. Drain.

Heat 1 tablespoon oil in a claypot till smoky. Sauté ginger and garlic till brown. Add in spring onions, Spanish onions, green pepper and carrot and fry for 2 minutes. Include seasoning.

Then add the deep-fried chicken and mix well. Fry for 5 minutes and then add 375 ml (1½ cups) water. Cover lid and bring ingredients to a boil. Then lower heat and allow to simmer for about 30 minutes or until all the liquid has been absorbed.

Switch off heat and serve in the claypot immediately.

淡
菜
燗
猪
尾 ☯

PIG'S TAIL WITH MUSSELS

2 pig's tails
50 g (2 oz) raw peanuts, soaked overnight
50 g (2 oz) dried mussels, soaked and cleaned
8 dried Chinese mushrooms, soaked in 750 ml (3 cups) water
6 red dates, stoned and rinsed
3 slices old ginger
1 tablespoon oil
1 teaspoon oyster sauce

MARINADE FOR PIG'S TAIL
1 teaspoon salt
1 teaspoon sugar
1 teaspoon light soya sauce
1 teaspoon dark soya sauce
2 tablespoons cornflour
1 tablespoon oil

MARINADE FOR MUSHROOMS
½ teaspoon salt
½ teaspoon sugar
½ teaspoon light soya sauce
½ teaspoon dark soya sauce
1 tablespoon cornflour
1 tablespoon oil

CORNFLOUR THICKENING
2 tablespoons cornflour
2 tablespoons water

My grandmother was the one who made sure that we ate different parts of animals according to the Chinese belief that eating a part of an animal would benefit the corresponding part of your body.

Naturally, she had a lot to say about eating pig's tails! Of course she did not say that we would grow tails after eating it, but she did say that pig's tail would strengthen our lumbar and ligaments.

In particular, this stew is good for blood circulation and strengthening the bone marrow.

Wash pig's tail and cut into 8 cm (3 inches) segments. Marinate for 15 minutes.

Squeeze out excess water from mushrooms. Trim stems. Retain water. Marinate mushrooms. Drain peanuts and mussels.

Heat 1 tablespoon of oil in claypot. When smoking, sauté ginger till fragrant.

Put in mushrooms and fry for 3 minutes. Then include pig's tail and fry for 5 minutes. Add peanuts. Pour in mushroom water and bring to a boil for 10 minutes. Lower flame and stew ingredients for 1 hour.

Now put in mussels and red dates and continue to stew for another hour. Season the dish with 1 teaspoon oyster sauce.

Thicken by stirring in 2 tablespoons of cornflour rendered in 2 tablespoons of water. Cook for 2 minutes before serving in the claypot.

草菇燜雞

STEWED CHICKEN WITH STRAW MUSHROOMS

40 g (1.3 oz) dried straw mushrooms
½ small chicken (0.5 kg, 1 lb), cut into serving pieces
½ carrot, skinned and sliced thickly
2 slices old ginger
20 g (0.7 oz) cloud fungus (*wan yee*)
1 tablespoon oil
½ teaspoon salt
½ teaspoon sugar

MARINADE FOR CHICKEN
1 teaspoon sugar
1 teaspoon light soya sauce
1 teaspoon Chinese rice wine
1 teaspoon ginger juice
½ teaspoon dark soya sauce
1 tablespoon oyster sauce

FOR SCALDING STRAW MUSHROOMS
2 slices old ginger
1 stalk spring onion
1.3 litres (5 cups) water

CORNFLOUR THICKENING
1 tablespoon cornflour
1 tablespoon water

This dish is good for tired bodies and I cook this stew once in a while to combat fatigue.

Straw mushrooms and cloud fungus have 'yin' properties. Cooked with chicken, which has 'yang' elements, the combination is perfectly balanced.

My mother always reminded me to scald dried straw mushrooms with ginger slices before cooking them. This, she said, was to cut down the 'cooling' properties of the mushroom.

Soak straw mushrooms in 600 ml (3 cups) warm water for 30 minutes. Squeeze out excess water. Keep mushroom water for later use.

Soak cloud fungus in warm water for 30 minutes. Squeeze off excess water. Discard water.

Marinate chicken for 15 minutes.

Bring scalding solution to a boil. Put in mushrooms to boil for 2 minutes. Drain and discard water, spring onions and ginger.

Heat 1 tablespoon oil in a claypot. When smoky, add ginger and fry till fragrant. Include straw mushrooms, carrots and cloud fungus and sauté for 5 minutes. Add in ½ teaspoon salt and ½ teaspoon sugar.

Now put in marinated chicken and fry for 5 minutes. Pour in 600 ml mushroom water and bring contents to a boil. Lower flame and simmer for 20 minutes. Lastly, pour in cornflour thickening and boil for 1 minute. Serve hot.

爛豬腳筋

STEWED MUSHROOMS WITH PIG'S TENDONS

Pig's tendons, if eaten regularly, can improve one's muscle condition, so if you need a dish to strengthen weak muscles and joints, this recipe is just right for you.

Dried pig's tendons are available from Chinese dried goods stores.

40 g (1.3 oz) Chinese dried mushrooms
50 g (2 oz) dried pig tendons
30 g (1 oz) sliced Chinese ham
6 red dates, stoned and rinsed
2 heads Chinese white cabbage (*pak choy*)
½ carrot, skinned and sliced
3 slices old ginger
2 tablespoons oil
1 teaspoon Chinese rice wine

MARINADE
½ teaspoon salt
1 teaspoon sugar
½ teaspoon cornflour
1 tablespoon oil

SEASONING
1 tablespoon oyster sauce
1 teaspoon sugar
½ teaspoon light soya sauce

THICKENING
2 tablespoons cornflour
4 tablespoons water
1 teaspoon dark soya sauce

Soak tendons in water overnight. Boil in water until tender. Rinse and drain. Remove stems and soak mushrooms in 750 ml (3 cups) of water for 30 minutes. Squeeze off excess water. Retain water. Marinate mushrooms for 15 minutes. Scald ham in hot water for 2 minutes.

Heat 2 tablespoons of oil in a pot. When the oil is smoky, sauté ginger till fragrant. Add carrots and fry for 2 minutes. Include mushrooms, tendons, red dates and ham. Fry for a further 5 minutes.

Pour in mushroom water. Bring to a boil and keep boiling for 10 minutes. Add the seasoning of oyster sauce, soya sauce and sugar. Lower flame and stew ingredients for 1½ hours.

Wash and cut cabbage. Blanch in boiling water for 2 minutes and drain. Add vegetables to pot during the last 5 minutes of cooking time. Thicken stew with cornflour mixture and stir briskly for 1 minute. Highlight with 1 teaspoon of Chinese rice wine before serving.

燜
釀
節
瓜
◐

STEWED STUFFED HAIRY MARROWS

2 hairy marrows
10 g (0.3 oz) Chinese dried mushrooms
3 dried scallops (approx. 30 g, 1 oz)
½ small carrot
120 g (4 oz) minced pork
1 tablespoon cornflour, rendered in 2 tablespoons water
1 teaspoon salt
1 teaspoon sugar
250 ml (1 cup) warm water
2 tablespoons oil

SEASONING FOR SAUCE
1 tablespoon oyster sauce
½ teaspoon salt
½ teaspoon sugar

CORNFLOUR THICKENING
2 tablespoons cornflour
4 tablespoons water

If you are in doubt as to which vegetable is suitable for your child who has indigestion and loss of appetite, then let me tell you that hairy marrow is a good choice.

Hairy marrows are considered to be 'neutral', possessing a balance of 'yin' and 'yang' elements. They are also easily digestible and therefore suitable for young children.

Wash and soak mushrooms in 125 ml (½ cup) warm water for 30 minutes. Squeeze off excess water. Reserve mushroom water for stock. Trim stems and dice mushrooms finely.

Wash and soak dried scallops in 125 ml (½ cup) warm water for 30 minutes. Drain, but keep water for stock. Chop scallops coarsely.

Skin hairy marrows. Clean and cut the marrows into 3 cm (1½ inch) rounds. Scoop out most of the pith and seeds for each round, leaving a well for stuffing.

Skin carrot and dice finely.

Mix minced pork with diced mushrooms, carrots and scallops. Add 1 teaspoon salt and 1 teaspoon sugar. Mix well.

Stuff rounds of marrow with filling and smooth cornflour thickening on top to keep stuffing in place. Place stuffed marrows on a dish and steam for 45 minutes.

Drain stock produced from steaming process. Combine this stock with mushroom water and scallop water.

Heat 2 tablespoons oil in a wok. Add stock and seasonings for sauce. Bring to a boil over high heat. Add the cornflour thickening and stir well for 1 minute. Pour gravy over cooked marrow rounds. Serve hot.

八寶盒 ●

EIGHT TREASURE BOX

1 dried beancurd sheet (fu pei)
300 g (10.5 oz) mini Chinese
  cabbage (siew pak choy)
6 pieces dried mushrooms
20 g (0.7 oz) dried scallops
10 g (0.3 oz) dried sea moss
160 g (6 oz) dried chestnuts
20 g (0.7 oz) barley, rinsed

80 g (3 oz) carrot, skinned and diced
80 g (3 oz) kale (kai lan), diced
8 red dates, stoned and rinsed
80 g (3 oz) pre-soaked lotus seeds,
  skinned and rinsed
2 slices old ginger
1 tablespoon oil
1.5 litres (6 cups) water

SEASONING
1 teaspoon salt
1 teaspoon sugar

SAUCE INGREDIENTS
250 ml (1 cup) mushroom and scallop water
2 tablespoons oyster sauce

CORNFLOUR THICKENING
1 tablespoon cornflour
2 tablespoons water

BLANCHING SOLUTION FOR CABBAGE
1.1 litres (4½ cups) boiling water
1 teaspoon salt
1 teaspoon oil

The eight treasures in this dish are mushrooms, chestnuts, barley, carrots, kale, lotus seeds, red dates and sea moss. They are all delicacies in traditional Chinese cuisine.

If you wish to entertain vegetarian guests with an exotic dish, this nutritious and colourful stew is perfect. However, remember to omit the dried scallops used to give the dish a more distinctive flavour if your guests are faithful vegetarians.

Soak dried chestnuts in warm water for 1 hour. Steam for 30 minutes. Keep chestnuts whole.

Trim stems from mushrooms and soak in 200 ml (1 cup) water for 30 minutes. Squeeze off excess water and dice. Retain mushroom water for sauce. Rinse and soak scallops in 200 ml water for 30 minutes. Tear into thin strips. Drain and retain water for sauce. Soak sea moss in water for 30 minutes. Remove grit and squeeze off excess water. Discard water. Bring 750 ml (3 cups) water to a boil. Add in barley and simmer for 15 minutes or until soft.

Heat 1 tablespoon oil in a wok. When smoky, add in ginger and fry till fragrant. Include mushrooms, carrot and kale and fry for 3 minutes. Then add in red dates, lotus seeds and chestnuts. Fry for another 2 minutes.

Put in the barley, sea moss and scallops. Add seasoning and fry for 2 minutes. Include half (250 ml, 1 cup) of the mushroom and scallop water. Cover and bring to a boil. Lower heat and stew for 30 minutes until mixture thickens.

Wipe beancurd sheet with a wet towel. Place in a deep bowl and ladle in stewed ingredients. Fold in the edges to make a packet. Place bowl in steamer and steam for 10 minutes.

Clean, wash and drain cabbage. Bring blanching solution to a boil ab blanch cabbage for 2 minutes. Drain and discard water.

Bring sauce ingredients to a boil. Add cornflour thickening and stir briskly for 1 minute. Transfer steamed packet carefully onto a serving plate and surround with cabbage. Use scissors to cut a big cross on packet and pull flaps back. Pour sauce over stuffing and cabbage. Serve.

白
雲
猪
手
◐

STEWED SWEET SOUR PIG'S TROTTERS

2 pig's fore-trotters, about 1 kg (2.2 lb)
100 g (3.5 oz) young ginger roots, shredded
200 g (7 oz) cucumber, pith removed, shredded
750 ml (3 cups) hot water

MARINADE FOR PICKLES
2 teaspoons salt
2 teaspoons sugar

PICKLING SOLUTION
2 teaspoons salt
8 tablespoons sugar
2 teaspoons white vinegar
1.5 litres (6 cups) water

The springs at the foothills of White Cloud Mountain 白云山 in Canton are famous for their purity.

The residents nearby used to stew pig's trotters until they were soft and tender. They would then put them in cloth bags which they secured to the rocks in the mountain streams. When all traces of grease had been rinsed from the pig's trotters by the cold, clear water, the trotters were taken home and pickled in a sweet and sour solution. This is why the Chinese still call this stew White Cloud Pig's Trotters.

This dish is an effective appetiser and good for strengthening muscles and joints.

Clean the trotters and remove hairs, if any. Chop into big pieces. Blanch in 1.5 litres (6 cups) boiling water for 5 minutes, drain and rinse well.

Bring another 1.5 litres (6 cups) of water to a boil, add the blanched trotters and stew over low flame for 45 minutes. Now remove the stewed trotters and rinse under a running tap to remove grease. Discard the liquid and wash pot clean.

Bring yet another 1.5 litres (6 cups) of water to a boil. Put in the stewed trotters and stew again over low flame for 30 minutes. Discard liquid and rinse trotters again under a running tap for 3 minutes to remove remaining grease. Soak trotters in ice-cold water for 30 minutes. Drain and discard water.

Marinate ginger and cucumber for 30 minutes. Rinse with 750 ml (3 cups) hot water and squeeze vegetables dry. Put aside.

Boil the pickling solution in a saucepan for 5 minutes. Adjust seasoning to suit taste and leave to cool for 30 minutes. Add the vegetables and mix evenly.

When the solution is cool, immerse the stewed trotters in the pickling solution and leave to stand for 2 hours. Serve warm or cold.

TO SERVE COLD: *Put the pot of pickled trotters in the refrigerator and chill for 8 hours. Remove from refrigerator and leave to stand at room temperature for 30 minutes before serving.*

STEWED SEA CUCUMBER & DUCK

海參燗鴨 ●

1 duck (2 kg, 4.4 lb)
3 pre-soaked sea cucumbers
10 dried Chinese mushrooms
1 carrot, skinned and wedged
½ can bamboo shoot, rinsed and wedged
2 stalks Chinese lettuce (sang choy)
2 slices old ginger
2 tablespoons oil
1.9 litres (7½ cups) oil

This is a good dish to serve on festive days and at parties since the whole duck will feed quite a number of people.

The best part of this stew is the Chinese lettuce which soaks up the nutritious sauce of the dish. Bamboo shoots, possessing 'yin' elements, give a hint of crunchiness to this stew which is good for replenishing the 'yin' essence and revitalising the blood.

MARINADE
2 teaspoons salt
2 teaspoons light soya sauce
1 teaspoon dark soya sauce

FOR SCALDING SEA CUCUMBERS
3 stalks spring onion
3 slices old ginger
1.9 litres (7½ cups) water

SEASONING
1 teaspoon salt
1 teaspoon sugar
1 tablespoon oyster sauce
1 tablespoon oil

CORNFLOUR THICKENING
2 tablespoons cornflour
2 tablespoons water
1 teaspoon dark soya sauce

Soak mushrooms in 1.5 litres (6 cups) of water for 30 minutes. Squeeze off excess water and trim stems. Retain mushroom water.

Gut, clean and wash duck thoroughly. Marinate.

Heat 1.5 litres of oil in a wok. When hot, deep fry duck for 5 minutes. Ladle out and drain.

Bring scalding liquid for sea cucumber to a boil. Put in sea cucumber and boil for 5 minutes. Drain and cut sea cucumber into big wedges. Discard scalding liquid.

Heat 2 tablespoons oil in a pot. When the oil is smoky, add ginger and fry till fragrant. Pour in mushroom water and bring to a boil.

Place the duck in the pot. Stew for 2 hours over low flame, then add sea cucumber and seasoning.

Add in mushrooms, carrot and bamboo shoots and stew for 30 minutes. Add cornflour thickening and stir briskly for 1 minute.

Wash and drain lettuce. Arrange lettuce on a platter and put duck in the centre of the plate. Surround the duck with sea cucumber and vegetables and pour gravy over the duck. Serve hot.

STEWED SPICY CHICKEN GIBLETS

滷
鷄
什
○

If you feel that serving chicken giblets to guests is offensive, let me explain that it is no different from serving calf's liver or steak and kidney pie.

My father even served these spicy giblets as an appetiser in his restaurant. He said they stimulate the appetite and strengthen the liver and kidneys.

Give this dish a try. Use salt to rub and clean the offals before cooking. The spicy stock in this recipe also helps to enhance the bland taste of the giblets.

4 chicken livers
4 chicken gizzards
1 stalk coriander leaves
1 teaspoon salt

SPICE STOCK
4 cloves
2 slices liquorice
5 g (0.15 oz) fennel seeds
5 g (0.15 oz) white peppercorns
10 g (0.3 oz) cinnamon sticks
4 star anise
1 teaspoon salt
4 tablespoons sugar
1.5 litres (6 cups) water

Clean and wash chicken livers and gizzards. Rub with 1 teaspoon salt. Rinse and drain.

Bring spice stock to a boil and simmer for 30 minutes over low heat. Sieve and discard the spices.

Bring the spice stock to a boil again. Add the gizzards and livers and stew over low flame for 1 hour or until giblets are tender.

Ladle out gizzards and livers and leave spicy stock to cool. (Do not serve the spicy stock but keep it for other recipes.)

Slice giblets and garnish with shredded coriander leaves. Serve.

STEWED DRIED SEAFOOD IN CLAYPOT

海味窩
●

6 dried scallops, about 30 g (1 oz)
10 g (0.3 oz) dried sea moss
8 dried Chinese mushrooms
6 dried Chinese mushrooms
6 dried oysters
400 g (14 oz) Tientsin cabbage (*wong nga bak*),
   cut into 8 cm (3 inch) pieces
½ small carrot, sliced
2 slices old ginger
2 shallots, sliced
2 tablespoons oil

SEASONING
½ teaspoon salt
1 teaspoon sugar
1 teaspoon light soya sauce
1 teaspoon dark soya sauce
1 tablespoon oyster sauce

CORNFLOUR THICKENING
1 tablespoon cornflour
2 tablespoons water

Of all the seasonal vegetables Chinese cooks add to their stews to soak up all the nutritional gravy, Tientsin cabbage is the favourite choice.

A late summer vegetable from Hebei province in Northern China, it is commonly preserved and pickled for the cold winter months.

Even in Singapore, Grandmother used to hang heads of the cabbage high above the kitchen to wind dry them for a couple of days. This natural dehydration, which rids the vegetable of its rawness, makes a great difference to its taste.

This stew has the effect of replenishing 'yin' essence and also benefits the kidneys.

Soak sea moss in warm water for 30 minutes. Squeeze excess water from sea moss. Rinse and soak scallops in 375 ml (1½ cups) warm water for 30 minutes. Retain scallop water. Trim off mushroom stems and soak mushrooms in 375 ml (1½ cups) warm water for 30 minutes. Squeeze off excess water and retain mushroom water. Wash and soak dried oysters in water for 30 minutes. Remove grit and discard water.

Bring 2.3 litres (9 cups) of water to a boil. Add cabbage and boil over medium flame for 30 minutes or until soft. Drain.

Heat 2 tablespoons oil in a claypot. When the oil is smoky, fry the ginger and shallots till fragrant. Then add in the mushrooms and carrots and fry for another 5 minutes.

Now include the oysters and scallops and fry for another 2 minutes. Pour in the scallop and mushroom water and bring to a boil. Lower heat and stew ingredients for about 1 hour or until about 375 ml (1½ cups) stock is left in the pot.

Add in the cabbage, sea moss and seasoning. Continue to stew for another 15 minutes. Add the cornflour thickening and stir. Allow to cook for a further 2 minutes. Check and adjust seasoning before serving.

紅燒鴨掌 ●

BRAISED DUCK'S WEBS

12 duck's webs
12 dried Chinese mushrooms
1 clove garlic, chopped
1 shallot, chopped
2 slices old ginger, chopped
2 tablespoons oil
1 teaspoon Chinese rice wine
1.5 litres (6 cups) oil
2 stalks spring onions, cut into 5 cm (2 inch) lengths
1 teaspoon salt

SEASONING	MARINADE FOR MUSHROOMS
1 teaspoon salt	1 teaspoon salt
1 teaspoon sugar	1 teaspoon sugar
1 teaspoon light soya sauce	½ teaspoon light soya sauce
1 teaspoon dark soya sauce	½ teaspoon dark soya sauce
1 tablespoon oyster sauce	1 tablespoon cornflour
1 tablespoon cornflour	1 tablespoon oil
1 tablespoon oil	

CORNFLOUR THICKENING
1 tablespoon cornflour
2 tablespoons water

One of the traditional Chinese concepts about food is that in choosing ingredients, one should choose ingredients according to the positive characteristics they exhibit. For example, ducks can both swim and walk, so their webs are considered to be strong – and therefore good – for strengthening the weak leg joints and muscles.

This is a 'yin' essence dish which is tender and gelatinous in texture.

Trim off mushroom stems and soak mushrooms in 750 ml (3 cups) warm water for 30 minutes. Squeeze off excess water and marinate for 10 minutes. Retain mushroom water.

Trim and clean duck's webs. Rub with 1 teaspoon salt and rinse thoroughly. Drain and dry. Bring 1.5 litres (6 cups) oil to a boil and deep-fry duck's webs for 3 minutes till lightly brown. Drain.

Heat 2 tablespoons oil in a claypot till very hot. Fry garlic, shallots and ginger till fragrant. Then include the mushrooms and fry well for 3 minutes. Add in the duck's webs and fry for another 5 minutes.

Pour in the mushroom water and bring to a boil. Lower heat and stew ingredients for 1 hour or until duck's webs are tender and a little liquid is left in the pot. Add seasoning. Include cornflour thickening and stir for 1 minute. Add spring onions and sprinkle in 1 teaspoon Chinese rice wine before serving. Serve hot.

STEWED HERBAL CHICKEN

½ large chicken (1 kg, 2.2 lb)
20 g (0.7 oz) sliced anglelica (*tong kwai*)
10 g (0.3 oz) medlar seeds (*kei chee*)
20 g (0.7 oz) dioscorea (*wai san*), soaked overnight
20 g (0.7 oz) astragalus (*puk kay*)
10 g (0.3 oz) dried longan flesh
2 tablespoons oil
600 ml (3 cups) hot water

SEASONING
1 teaspoon salt
1 tablespon wine
1 teaspoon light soya sauce

CORNFLOUR THICKENING
1 tablespoon cornflour
2 tablespoons water

MARINADE
½ teaspoon salt
½ teaspoon sugar
½ teaspoon light soya sauce
1 tablespoon cornflour
1 tablespoon oil

Clean and wash chicken thoroughly. Cut into big pieces and marinate for 15 minutes. Rinse herbs.

Heat 2 tablespoons of oil in a pot. When the oil is hot, sauté marinated chicken for 5 minutes. Add herbs and fry for 1 minute.

Pour in 750 ml (3 cups) of hot water to cover the ingredients and bring to a boil. Lower flame and stew for 1½ hours. Remember to check the water level occasionally. Add seasoning.

Stir in cornflour thickening 2 minutes before serving. Serve hot.

I cook this herbal stew to pep up blood circulation and improve general health. Of the main ingredients, anglelica (tong kwai) *feeds the blood while* astragalus (puk kay) *helps fortify blood circulation. This dish is therefore helpful to those suffering from anemia.*

苦
瓜
燜
燒
鴨

STEWED ROAST DUCK WITH BITTERGOURD

½ roasted duck (1 kg, 2.2 lb)
1 large bittergourd
3 slices old ginger
2 cloves garlic, crushed
1 piece preserved tangerine peel, soaked and drained
1 red chilli (optional), cut into big slices
375 ml (1½ cups) water
2 tablespoons oil

MARINADE
½ teaspoon salt
½ teaspoon sugar

SEASONING
1 teaspoon salt
1 teaspoon sugar
2 tablespoons oil

The older folks in my family can be counted on to create recipes to suit particular body compositions.

Take this recipe for example. A person with a dominant 'yin' body composition should not eat bittergourd which has 'cooling' properties. But if such as person loves bittergourd, then it is possible for him or her to enjoy the gourd if it is cooked with a 'heaty' food to achieve a balance between 'yin' and 'yang' properties. The choice here is roasted duck, since ducks, after roasting, are 'heaty'.

Cut the roasted duck into serving pieces.

Remove seeds from bittergourd and cut gourd into 3 cm (1 inch) slices. Marinate bittergourd in 2 teaspoons salt and 1 teaspoon sugar for 15 minutes. Rinse with hot water and drain.

Heat 2 tablespoons oil in a pot. When the oil is smoky, add ginger and garlic and fry till fragrant. Add roasted duck and fry for 5 minutes.

Put in bittergourd and seasoning. Fry for a further 5 minutes then add tangerine peel.

Pour in 375 ml (1½ cup) of water. Bring ingredients to a boil and keep boiling for 10 minutes. Lower flame and stew for 1 hour.

Stir in cornflour thickening 1 minute before serving. Garnish with sliced chilli and serve.

STEWED HAIRY MARROW
WITH MUNGBEAN VERMICELLI

大姨媽嫁女

1 hairy marrow
50 g (2 oz) dried shrimps (*har mai*)
200 g (7 oz) mungbean vermicelli (*fun see*)
2 slices old ginger
1 shallot, sliced
1 garlic, sliced
1 tablespoon oil

SEASONING
1 teaspoon salt
1 teaspoon sugar
1 teaspoon light soya sauce

Skin hairy marrow. Wash and dry. Slice at a slant into matchstick-sized strips.

Wash and soak dried shrimps in 375 ml (1½ cups) warm water for 30 minutes. Remove any bits of shell and drain. Retain water.

Soak mungbean vermicelli in warm water for 30 minutes. Drain. Cut into 8 cm (3 inch) lengths.

Heat 1 tablespoon oil in a wok until hot. Fry ginger, shallots and garlic till fragrant. Stir in dried shrimps and continue frying for 3 minutes.

Add marrow sticks and seasoning; fry for 5 minutes. Pour in the shrimp water and bring to a boil. Lower heat and leave to stew for 10 minutes.

Lastly, add in the soaked mungbean vermicelli and continue to stew for another 15 minutes until ingredients are cooked and soggy. Check seasoning and serve immediately.

Mungbean vermicelli are made from ground mung beans and are sold fresh in Long Hou (Dragon Mouth City) in Shantung province. For export, the bean vermicelli are dried and tied into small bundles and sealed in plastic bags.

Best quality bean vermicelli are very dry, fine and almost transparent. This is why they are also popularly known as transparent vermicelli.

The Cantonese have a nickname for this dish – Marriage of Eldest Aunt's Daughter (tai yee ma kor loi). The story goes that so-and-so's eldest aunt could not afford a shark's fin dish for her daughter's marriage feast, so she used bean vermicelli as a substitute. In the process, she created this economical, but exciting new dish.

I like this dish as it stimulates the appetite, especially with the slippery smooth bean thread having absorbed the flavours of the other ingredients.

髮
菜
魚
丸
窩
◐

STEWED FISHBALLS WITH SEA MOSS

400 g (14 oz) fish paste
20 g (0.7 oz) sea moss (fatt choy)
2 slices old ginger, shredded
2 stalks spring onions, shredded
1 small head iceburg lettuce, about 300 g (10.5 oz)
3 tablespoons oil
1 tablespoon cornflour

SEASONING
1 teaspon salt
1 teaspoon sugar
½ teaspoon light soya sauce
½ teaspoon dark soya sauce
1 tablespoon oyster sauce
Dash of pepper
150 ml (¾ cup) hot water

SALT SOLUTION
½ teaspoon salt
2 tablespoons water

CORNFLOUR THICKENING
1 teaspoon cornflour
1 tablespoon water

It is very convenient nowadays to buy fresh prepared fish paste from Asian markets. In the past, housewives made the fish paste themselves and those who could produce good fish paste prided themselves on it. My grandmother was one such expert.

It was fun to watch grandmother make fish paste. First, she used a spoon to scrape off the flesh of the fish. Then she used the blade of a cleaver to flatten the fish meat on a chopping board. After that, the pressed fish meat was put inside a big basin and she used her hands to knead and throw the meat against the side of the basin. Salt water was sprinkled in during the beating process to bind the fish flesh into a paste and this kneading and beating would continue for ten minutes till the paste became springy to the touch. Finally, she would squeeze quanitities of the paste through her thumb and forefinger to make the fishballs or keep the paste for other recipes.

Grandmother had a sure way of getting rid of the fishy smell from her hands. She would first rinse her hands and then rub in lime or lemon juice before soaking her hands in a bowl of warm Chinese tea for a couple of minutes.

Soak sea moss in water for 15 minutes. Drain and squeeze off excess water. Wash and drain lettuce. Separate the leaves.

Put fish paste in a big bowl. Take handfuls of the paste and throw it against the side of the bowl till the paste becomes springy. Sprinkle in salt solution between beats.

Add sea moss to fish paste and mix evenly. Form the mixture into 3-cm (1-inch) balls. Dredge lightly with cornflour.

Heat 2 tablespoons oil in a claypot. When smoky, add in fishballs and fry for 5 minutes until cooked. Drain and put fishballs aside.

Reheat claypot with 1 tablespoon oil. Add in ginger and spring onions and fry till fragrant. Put in the seasoning and 150 ml (¾ cups) hot water and bring to boil.

Include the fishballs and leave to simmer for 5 minutes, then add lettuce and cook for another 2 minutes.

Add the cornflour thickening and stir for 2 minutes. Serve hot.

紅燒魚頭 ☯

STEWED GROUPER HEAD

½ grouper head

6 dried Chinese mushrooms, soaked in 600 ml (3 cups) water

3 slices old ginger

6 cloves garlic, lightly crushed

50 g (2 oz) roasted pork belly

½ carrot, skinned and sliced

50 g (2 oz) cauliflower, cut into florets

2 stalks spring onions, cut into 5 cm (2 inch) lengths

1 stalk Chinese lettuce (sang choy), washed and drained

20 g (0.7 oz) snow peas, deveined

1 big green pepper (capsicum), deseeded and cut into wedges

2.3 litres (9 cups) oil

2 tablespoons cornflour

3 teaspoon salt

1 teaspoon sugar

1 tablespoon oyster sauce

1 tablespoon oil

CORNFLOUR THICKENING
2 tablespoons cornflour
2 tablespoons water
1 teaspoon dark soya sauce

MARINADE FOR MUSHROOMS
¼ teaspoon salt
¼ teaspoon sugar
¼ teaspoon cornflour

One rule of Chinese cooking is: waste nothing in the kitchen. So, a grouper head becomes the main ingredient for this dish.

If the head is deep-fried well, its skin and bones become crispy and are delicious. In fact, eating fish bones will add calcium and other minerals to your diet.

Clean and wash fish head thoroughly. Wipe dry with kitchen towel. Rub 2 teaspoons of salt all over fish head. Leave to stand for 15 minutes. Rinse and wipe dry again. Coat evenly with 2 tablespoons of cornflour.

Heat 1.5 litre oil in wok. When sizzling hot, put in the coated fish head to deep fry each side for 10 minutes until golden brown. Drain and set aside.

Squeeze excess water from mushrooms and trim stems. Retain water. Marinate the mushrooms with ¼ teaspoon each of salt, sugar and cornflour.

Heat claypot with 1 teaspoon of oil. When hot, sauté ginger and garlic until fragrant. Add marinated mushrooms, pork belly and fry for 5 minutes. Now put in carrots and cauliflowers. Include 1 teaspoon salt, 1 teaspoon sugar and 600 ml (3 cups) of mushroom water.

Bring to a boil and keep boiling for 15 minutes. Lower flame and stew ingredients for 30 minutes. Add snow peas, green pepper, spring onion and 1 tablespoon oyster sauce. Include cornflour thickening. Immerse deep-fried fish head in the stew for 5 minutes before serving.

Wash and drain lettuce. Line serving platter with lettuce and ladle fish head onto centre of plate. Pour stewed vegetables and gravy over it.

Serve hot.

木耳燗鷄○

STEWED CHICKEN WITH WOOD FUNGUS

½ small chicken (0.5 kg, 1 lb)
10 g (0.3 oz) dried lily buds (*kum chum*)
10 g (0.3 oz) wood fungus (*mok yee*)
10 g (0.3 oz) dried Chinese mushrooms
6 red dates, stoned and rinsed
2 slices old ginger
1 tablespoon oil

MARINADE
1 teaspoon salt
1 teaspoon sugar
½ teaspoon light soya sauce
½ teaspoon dark soya sauce
1 tablespoon ginger juice
2 tablespoons cornflour
1 tablespoon oil

My grandmother advised me to slow down each time she noticed that I had symptoms of stress. But how? "Well, by eating the right things, of course," she said. And that's how I got to know this stew which has the effect of improving blood circulation and reducing stess.

Grandmother's choice of ingredients for this stew was spot on. Wood fungus improves blood circulation while dried lily buds are rich in minerals and have a calming effect.

Soak mushrooms in 375 ml (1½ cup) water for 30 minutes. Squeeze excess water and trim stems. Reserve the mushroom water for later use.

Soak lily buds in water for 15 minutes. Squeeze dry and knot two buds together at the centre. Soak wood fungus in water for 30 minutes. Drain and cut into small pieces.

Wash and cut chicken into serving pieces. Marinate for 15 minutes.

Heat a tablespoon oil in a wok. When the oil is smoky, add ginger and fry till fragrant.

Include wood fungus and mushrooms and fry for another 2 minutes, then add red dates.

Put in marinated chicken and fry for 5 minutes. Add mushroom water, cover wok and cook for 10–15 minutes.

Add lily buds during the last 5 minutes of cooking time. Serve hot.

STEWED CHESTNUTS WITH CHICKEN

栗子燜鷄 ○

1 medium-sized chicken (1.5 kg, 3.3 lb)
800 (1.8 lb) shelled Chinese chestnuts
1 slice old ginger
1 tablespoon oil
600 ml (3 cups) water

MARINADE
1 teaspoon salt
1 teaspoon light soya sauce
1 tablespoon cornflour
1 tablespoon dark soya sauce
1 tablespoon vegetable oil
1 tablespoon oyster sauce

Late autumn heralds the arrival of chestnuts which are not only delicious but are also full of nutrition.

There are many types of chestnuts grown in China, but the best grade comes from Liang Xiang County in Hebei province.

Much as we like them, chestnuts should be eaten in moderation as they can cause indigestion and possess 'heaty' properties. However, it is also believed that chestnuts strengthen the spleen, stomach and kidneys.

Chestnuts have a delicate sweetness which is brought to its fullness here when cooked with chicken.

Wash chestnuts and boil in about 2 litres (8 cups) of water for 30 minutes. Discard water, rinse chestnuts and peel off membranes. Keep chestnuts whole.

Wash chicken and pat dry. Cut into serving pieces and marinate for 15 minutes.

Heat 1 tablespoon oil in a claypot. When oil is smoky, add ginger and fry for 1 minute. Put in chicken and sauté for 5 minutes. Include chestnuts and mix well.

Include 600 ml of water and bring to a boil for 10 minutes over high flame. Lower heat and simmer for 1 hour. Serve in the claypot.

蠔油鮑甫 ☯ STEWED ABALONE IN OYSTER SAUCE

4 dried abalones, about 400 g (14 oz)
300 g (10.5 oz) Chinese spinach (*por choy*)
2 bamboo mattings

SEASONING
½ teaspoon salt
1 teaspoon sugar
½ teaspoon light soya sauce
1 teaspoon dark soya sauce
Dash of pepper
1 tablespoon oil
1 tablespoon oyster sauce

SUPERIOR STOCK
½ chicken
2 pork ribs
3 dried scallops
200 g (7 oz) pork skin, hair removed
1.5 litres (9 cups) water

CORNFLOUR THICKENING
1 tablespoon cornflour
2 tablespoons water

BLANCHING SOLUTION FOR SPINACH
1.1 litres (4½ cups) boiling water
1 teaspoon salt
1 teaspoon oil

Abalone is a top grade seafood to the Chinese. Dried whole abalones, though rock hard and require a long cooking time to achieve the right texture and flavour, are very expensive. Canned abalones are much cheaper, with a sweet, soft texture and require only a very short cooking time. In fact, you can eat canned abalone straight out of the can.

My father enjoyed taking the time to prepare and cook dried abalone. He stressed that cooking dried abalone by the long method kept the nutrients of the ingredient. Mother, on the other hand, preferred to use canned abalone, saying that they were more economical and saved time. The choice is really yours.

This is a dish to serve during the lunar new year since the sound of the Chinese name for abalone – pao yu – is the same as the words which mean 'guaranteed excess prosperity.'

Soak the dried abalones in 1.5 litres (6 cups) water for 2 hours. Use a small brush to remove any sand and grit. Discard water. Put cleaned abalones in a clay pot with 1.5 litres (6 cups) water and bring it to a boil. Lower flame and continue to simmer for 30 minutes. Switch off heat and leave pot with cover on overnight. The next day, ladle out the abalones. Brush and clean again. Retain abalone water.

Put the bamboo mattings in a pot and place abalones on the matting to prevent them from sticking to the bottom of the pot. Include the reserved abalone water and bring to a boil. Lower heat and leave to stew for 4 hours, adding boiling water occasionally. When abalones becomes soft, drain and retain abalone water (about 375 ml, 1½ cups).

In the meantime, prepare superior stock by simmering stock ingredients over a low flame until 750 ml (3 cups) stock is obtained. Sieve stock and discard ingredients.

Heat a saucepan till very hot. Put in the superior stock, abalone water and abalones in that order. Stew over low heat for 2 hours until ¾ cup sauce is left.

Clean and wash spinach. Cut into 8 cm (3 inch) lengths. Bring blanching solution to a boil and blanch spinach. Drain and arrange the vegetables to cover a serving platter.

Ladle out the abalones and slice obliquely into thick slices. Arrange the abalone slices on top of blanched spinach.

Heat a wok till very hot. Pour in the prepared abalone sauce and seasoning. Bring to a boil. Add cornflour thickening and stir briskly for 2 minutes. Pour sauce over abalone and vegetables. Serve hot.

CANNED ABALONE STEWED IN OYSTER SAUCE

500 g (1.1 lb) canned abalone
500 g (1.1 lb) iceburg lettuce

SAUCE INGREDIENTS
1 teaspoon salt
2 teaspoons sugar
½ teaspoon light soya sauce
1 teaspoon dark soya sauce
1 tablespoon oyster sauce
1 tablespoon oil
300 ml (1½ cups) liquid from canned abalone

SEASONING
1 teaspoon Chinese rice wine
Dash of pepper

BLANCHING SOLUTION FOR LETTUCE
1.1 litres (4½ cups) boiling water
1 teaspoon salt
1 teaspoon oil

CORNFLOUR THICKENING
1 tablespoon cornflour
2 tablespoons water

Clean, wash and drain lettuce. Separate leaves. Bring blanching solution to a boil and blanch lettuce. Drain and arrange lettuce leaves on a serving platter.

Drain canned abalone and retain liquid for the sauce. Slice abalone thinly at an angle.

Bring sauce ingredients to a boil. Thicken with cornflour thickening and stir for 1 minute.

Add sliced abalone to the sauce and stir for 1 minute. Season with Chinese rice wine and pepper.

Ladle abalone onto lettuce and pour the sauce over the abalone.

Serve hot.

羌
蔥
焗
鯉
○

STEWED CARP WITH
SPRING ONION & GINGER

1 Chinese carp (lei yu), about 600 g (1.2 lb)
100 g (3.5 oz) old ginger, grated
3 stalks spring onions
3 tablespoons oil
1 teaspoon salt

SEASONING
2 teaspoons salt
2 teaspoons sugar
1 teaspoon light soya sauce
Dash of pepper

The carp is an auspcious symbol to the Chinese. Like the salmon, spawning carp are able to swim against strong currents and leap many feet out of water on their way upstream. This fact is reflected in a Chinese legend which has carps learping over the Dragon's Gate. No wonder the carp is always associated with strength and vitality in the Chinese mind.

The womenfolk of my family love this stew as it helps improve blood circulation. Even my father enjoyed eating it, especially the roe and milt. Also edible are the beautiful golden-black scales of the fish which shimmer in the sunlight like armour on a brave warrior. Beyond these, carps are commonly eaten for their succulent white flesh which is high in protein and minerals.

Gut, clean and wash carp. Retain roe if any. Rub the fish evenly with 1 teaspoon salt and marinate cavity with some grated ginger. Cut spring onions into 8 cm (3 inch) lengths.

Heat 3 tablespoons oil in a claypot until smoky. Sauté the spring onions and remaining grated ginger until fragrant.

Add in the carp (and roe, if any) and fry both sides of the fish till slightly golden brown.

Pour in 375 ml (1½ cups) water, cover and bring to a boil. Stew fish for 10 minutes over medium heat. Now, add seasoning and continue to cook for another 10 minutes. Check seasoning and adjust to taste.

If the sauce is thin, stir in 1 tablespoon cornflour rendered in 2 tablespoons water to thicken. Serve hot in claypot.

紅
燒
鮑
翅

BRAISED COMB SHARK'S FINS

500 g (1.1 lb) soaked comb shark's fins
10 g (0.3 oz) Chinese ham, minced
2 sheets bamboo matting
1 teaspoon Chinese rice wine
2 tablespoons red Chinese vinegar

SUPERIOR STOCK
½ chicken
2 pork ribs
3 dried scallops
200 g (7 oz) pork skin,
   hair removed
2.3 litres (9 cups) water

SCALDING LIQUID
4 slices old ginger
2 stalks spring onions
1 tablespoon Chinese rice wine
3 litres (12 cups) water

SEASONING
1 teaspoon salt
1 teaspoon sugar
½ teaspoon light soya sauce
1 teaspoon dark soya sauce
1 tablespoon oyster sauce
Dash of pepper

CORNFLOUR THICKENING
1 tablespoon cornflour
2 tablespoons water

Whole shark's fins, commonly known as comb shark's fin to the West, is 'pow chi' to the Cantonese. They are, by far, the most popular and expensive type of shark's fin which is actually the rear fin of the Great White Shark, made famous by the movie Jaws.

Never, never buy unprocessed dried shark's fins. They are very fishy and come with tough bones and rough skin. It would take you two to three days of messy work to prepare it for cooking.

Today, Chinese speciality stores offer dried or frozen processed whole shark's fins. To prepare processed dried whole fins, put them in a pot of boiling water and boil for 15 minutes. Switch off the heat and keeping the lid on, soak the shark's fin overnight. Drain and discard the water.

I prefer to use frozen shark's fins. All I need to do is thaw them and scald them to get rid of any remaining fishy smell before actual cooking.

Prepare stock by simmering stock ingredients over a low flame until 750 ml (3 cups) stock is obtained. Sieve stock and reserve.

Bring scalding liquid to a boil. Put soaked shark's fins between two bamboo mattings. Secure edges of matting with bamboo skewers or toothpicks so that the fins do not fall apart during preparation and cooking. Scald shark's fins for 1 hour.

Remove and soak the prepared shark's fins in fresh water for 30 minutes. Remove and drain.

Place the shark's fins in a big claypot. Pour in the prepared superior stock and bring it to a boil over a high flame. Lower flame to medium and stew shark's fins for 1 hour.

Remove the shark's fins from pot. Take shark's fins from bamboo matting and arrange the fins on a serving plate.

Heat a wok till very hot and sprinkle in 1 teaspoon Chinese rice wine. Add remaining stock from claypot and then include the seasoning. Bring this to a boil, then add cornflour thickening and stir briskly for 2 minutes. Remove the bamboo matting from the cooked shark's fins.

Pour sauce over the shark's fins and sprinkle minced Chinese ham on top. Serve with a small plate of red Chinese vinegar.

STEWED LOTUS ROOT WITH PIG'S TROTTERS

蓮藕燜豬蹄 ☯

This dish is one of my nanny's special-ties and I am glad that I learnt it from her. It is good for cleansing the blood and strengthening the joints.

Lotus roots and pig's trotters make a good combination but these hard-textured ingredients need a special seasoning like red fermented bean-curd to mellow them and enhance their mild flavours.

Red fermented beancurd (nam yu) is made from fresh beancurd fermented in salt, red rice grains and rice wine. This accounts for its colour and its strong cheesy taste.

1 pig's trotter, about 1 kg (2.2 lb)
2 sections lotus roots, about 1 kg (2.2 lb)
80 g (2.5 oz) red fermented yam curd (nam yu), mashed
2 slices old ginger
2 cloves garlic, bruised and skinned
1.1 litres (4½ cups) water
1 tablespoon oil

MARINADE FOR TROTTER
1 teaspoon salt
1 teaspoon sugar
1 teaspoon light soya sauce
1 teaspoon dark soya sauce
3 tablespoons cornflour
1 tablespoon oil

SEASONING (OPTIONAL)
1 teaspoon salt
1 teaspoon sugar

Clean the trotters and remove hairs, if any. Cut into big serving pieces. Marinate for 30 minutes.

Wash lotus roots thoroughly. Cut the root into 3 x 5 cm (1 x 2 inch) sections and bruise each section lightly with the flat of a cleaver.

Heat 1 tablespoon oil in a claypot. Add garlic and ginger and fry for 30 seconds. Include the red fermented yam curd and fry till fragrant.

Put in the marinated trotters and mix thoroughly for 5 minutes, then include the lotus root sections and fry, mixing well, for a further 5 minutes.

Now pour in 900 ml (4½ cups) water and cover lid. Bring to a boil and keep boiling for 10 minutes. Then lower heat and simmer ingredients for 1½ hours or until trotters are tender and very little liquid remains. Check seasoning before serving and adjust to your taste. Serve dish in the claypot with bowls of plain rice.

STEWED BEANCURD DELUXE

紅燒豆腐 ☯

400g (14 oz) beancurd (*tofu*)
6 dried Chinese mushrooms
50 g (2 oz) lean pork
20 g (0.7 oz) Chinese ham, sliced
40 g (1.4 oz) snow peas, deveined
50 g (2 oz) baby corn, halved
½ small carrot, skinned and sliced
2 slices old ginger
1 clove garlic, sliced
1 shallots, sliced
1.1 litres (4½ cups) oil
1 tablespoon oil

Chinese cooks use cured ham to flavour their dishes. Used in small quantities, thinly sliced or finely diced, they are subtly combined with other ingredients.

This beancurd stew is a good example of a well-balanced dish suitable for young and old. It is best eaten a few hours after cooking to allow the deep-fried beancurds to absorb the tasty gravy, but reheat the stew just before serving.

SEASONING
1 teaspoon salt
1 teaspoon sugar
1 teaspoon light soya sauce
½ teaspoon dark soya sauce
½ tablespoon oyster sauce
Dash of pepper

MARINADE FOR PORK
½ teaspoon salt
½ teaspoon sugar
1 teaspoon cornflour
1 teaspoon oil

CORNFLOUR THICKENING
1 tablespoon cornflour
2 tablespoons water

Drain and dry beancurd. Cut into 2 x 4 cm (1 x 1.5 inch) pieces. Heat 1.1 litres (4½ cups) of oil in a wok. When hot, slide in the the beancurd and deep-fry until golden brown (about 10 minutes). Remove and drain.

Trim mushroom stems and soak mushrooms in 375 ml (1½ cups) warm water for 30 minutes. Squeeze off excess water and retain mushroom water.

Rinse and dry pork and then slice thinly across the grain. Marinate for 15 minutes.

Pour all but 1 tablespoon oil from the wok. Reheat the oil and when smoky, fry the garlic, shallots and ginger till fragrant. Add in the carrot and mushrooms and fry for a further 5 minutes. Dish out and set aside.

Reheat wok with 1 tablespoon oil. When hot, put in the marinated pork and fry for 3 minutes. Add in the fried beancurd, Chinese ham, carrots and mushrooms and fry for another 1 minute.

Now pour in the mushroom water, cover lid and bring ingredients to a boil. Lower heat and leave to stew for 5 minutes or until there is about 250 ml (1¼ cups) liquid left in the wok. Add in the baby corn, snow peas and seasoning. Cook for 2 minutes. Add cornflour thickening and keep stirring for 2 minutes. Serve hot.

淡菜爛冬菇

MUSSELS WITH CARROT & MUSHROOMS

50 g (2 oz) dried mussels
10 dried Chinese mushrooms
1 carrot, skinned and wedged
5 g (0.3 oz) dried sea moss, soaked and drained
1 tablespoon oil

MARINADE
1 teaspoon salt
1 teaspoon sugar
1 teaspoon light soya sauce
1 tablespoon cornflour
1 tablespoon oil
½ teaspoon dark soya sauce

CORNFLOUR THICKENING
1 tablespoon cornflour
2 tablespoon water
½ teaspoon oyster sauce

A number of my students asked me what food is good for those who suffer from night sweats. I told them to try this stew.

During my childhood, when I perspired a lot in my sleep, Grandmother would say that it was an indication that my general health was poor. She would then cook this dish for me, and after several doses, my night sweat stopped completely.

Clean mussels and rinse. Soak mussels in 300 ml (1½ cups) of warm water for 1 hour. Drain, but retain water.

Soak mushrooms in 375 ml (1½ cups) of warm water for 30 minutes. Drain, squeeze out excess water and retain water for later use. Trim stems and marinate mushrooms.

Heat a claypot with 1 tablespoon oil. When the oil is smoky, add carrot wedges and marinated mushrooms. Sauté them for 5 minutes.

Pour in water from mushrooms and mussels and boil for 10 minutes. Include mussels and simmer over medium flame for 1 hour.

Put in sea moss 10 minutes before serving. Stir in cornflour thickening and cook for 2 minutes. Check seasoning and adjust to suit your taste. Serve hot.

麻
婆
豆
腐
○

MA POR TOFU

400 g (14 oz) soft bean curd (*tofu*)
100 g (3.5 oz) minced pork
30 g (1 oz) pickled mustard (*jar choy*)
2 stalks spring onions, chopped
1 red chilli, deseeded and diced
2 cloves garlic, chopped
1 tablespoon hot broad bean paste (*tau ban cheong*)
1 teaspoon Chinese rice wine
2 tablespoons oil
4 tablespoons water

MARINADE FOR PORK
½ teaspoon salt
½ teaspoon sugar
½ teaspoon light soya sauce
1 teaspoon oil
1 tablespoon cornflour

SEASONING
1 teaspoon sugar
1 teaspoon light soya sauce
½ teaspoon dark soya sauce
1 teaspoon sesame oil
Dash of pepper

CORNFLOUR THICKENING
1 tablespoon cornflour
2 tablespoons water

The ingredients which make this dish popular are the pickled mustard and the hot broad bean paste.

Pickled mustard is made from the swollen stem of a species of mustard from Szechuan province. First pickled in salt solution and then pressed dry, it is pickled again in a fine, red chilli powder. This chilli powder is rinsed off before the pickled mustard is used, but the vegetable remains salty and spicy hot, giving the tofu in this dish a sharp, peppery tang.

The distinctive taste of hot broad bean paste comes from crushed chilli, sugar and salt. It is very hot and spicy and is an indispensible ingredient for making this popular Szechuan dish.

Since this dish is both spicy and easily digestible, it is a favourite among old people.

Cut beancurd into 2 cm (1 inch) cubes. Drain. Marinate minced pork for 10 minutes. Wash pickled mustard briefly, then chop, rinse and drain.

Heat 2 tablespoons of oil in a wok. When hot, fry the chilli, garlic and the broad bean paste till fragrant. Now add the pickled mustard and then the minced pork.

Continue frying and sprinkle in 1 teaspoon Chinese rice wine and 4 tablespoons water.

Now put in the beancurd and seasoning. Leave to simmer for 2 minutes then add cornflour thickening. Keep stirring for 2 minutes and add the chopped spring onion. Serve hot.

HAPPY FAMILY

合家歡 🔵

This claypot stew is a popular dish among the Chinese during the festive season as it has a beautiful presentation, is nutritious and surprisingly easy to prepare.

The dish is known as Happy Family because it contains meat, poultry, soya products, vegetables and seafood – all the different types of ingredients used in Chinese cooking.

1 pre-soaked sea cucumber
200 g (7 oz) chicken fillet, wedged
100 g (3.5 oz) prawns, shelled and deveined
1 squid, about 100 g (3.5 oz), cut into thick rings
6 dried Chinese mushrooms
200 g (7 oz) soft beancurd (*tofu*)

50 g (2 oz) canned bamboo shoot
1 clove garlic, sliced
2 sliced old ginger
1 shallot, sliced
100 g (3.5 oz) carrot, skinned and sliced
100 g (3.5 oz) roasted pork belly, cut into thick slices
100 g (3.5 oz) snow peas, deveined
750 ml (3 cups) oil

FOR SCALDING SEA CUCUMBER
1 stalk spring onion
2 slices old ginger
1.1 litres (4½ cups) water

MARINADE FOR PRAWNS AND SQUIDS
½ teaspoon salt
½ teaspoon sugar
1 teaspoon oil

MARINADE FOR CHICKEN
¼ teaspoon salt
½ teaspoon sugar
½ teaspoon Chinese rice wine
¼ teaspoon soya sauce
1 teaspoon cornflour
1 teaspoon oil

SEASONING
1 teaspoon salt
1 teaspoon sugar
1 tablespoon oyster sauce
Dash of pepper

CORNFLOUR THICKENING
1 tablespoon cornflour
2 tablespoons water
½ teaspoon dark soya sauce

Trim off stems and soak mushrooms in 375 ml (1½ cups) warm water for 15 minutes. Squeeze off excess water. Retain mushrooms water.

Boil scalding solution and scald sea cucumber for 5 minutes. Discard the solution and rinse sea cucumber. Cut into 3 cm sections.

Marinate chicken for 10 minutes, and prawns and squid for 5 minutes.

Cut beancurd into 3 cm (1 inch) cubes. Deep-fry in 750 ml (3 cups) oil for 5 minutes until golden brown. Drain, retaining 1 tablespoon of oil.

Blanch bamboo shoots in 600 ml (3 cups) boiling water for 5 minutes. Rinse, drain and wedge.

Heat the retained oil in a claypot until smoky. Put in garlic, ginger and shallots and fry till fragrant. Add in the mushrooms, carrot, bamboo shoots and pork belly and fry for 3 minutes.

Pour in the mushroom water and bring to a boil. Add in marinated chicken, and sea cucumber, then stew over low heat for 5 minutes. Include fried beancurd, prawns, squids, snow peas and seasoning.

Thicken gravy with cornflour thickening and stir for 2 minutes. Serve hot in claypot.

好
市
發
財

STEWED PIG'S TROTTER WITH OYSTERS & MUSHROOMS

The name of this dish 好市发财 can be loosely translated as 'Prosperity in a Good Market'. With such a name, forget about calories and cholesterol because the Chinese regard names of dishes as important as the food itself. So long as the names convey propitious things, the food must be good.

You need to appreciate the puns between the names of the ingredients used in this dish and the festive sayings which convey good wishes during the Chinese New Year to fully understand why this dish is traditionally served at our family reuinion dinner. In fact, my parents carefully chose each ingredient for this, their version of the popular New Year stew. You will see that it is intended to bring all good things to the family.

Mushrooms (tong koo) stand for Tong Seng Sai Chou 东成西就 – Wishes Fulfilled from East to West. Lettuce (sang choy) and pig's trotter (jue sau) appear in Wang Choy Chou Sau 横财就手 – Luck Comes with All You Handle, or Midas touch without dire consequences. Lastly, dried oysters (hou si) and sea moss (fatt choy) pun perfectly with Hou Si Fatt Choy 好市发财 Prosperity in a Good Market.

Names aside, this stew is good for the stomach, feeding it well, and soothing it and the intestines.

1 roasted pig's trotter
  (siew jue sau)
12 dried Chinese mushrooms
8 dried oysters
10 g (0.3 oz) sea moss
½ carrot, skinned and sliced

500 g (1.1 lb) iceburg lettuce
1 shallot, crushed
1 clove garlic, crushed
2 slices old ginger
1 tablespoon oil
1 teaspoon Chinese rice wine

MARINADE FOR MUSHROOMS
1 teaspoon salt
1 teaspoon sugar
1 teaspoon light soya sauce
½ teaspoon dark soya sauce
2 tablespoons cornflour
1 tablespoon oil

SEASONING
1 tablespoon oyster sauce
2 teaspoon sugar
1 teaspoon dark soya sauce

CORNFLOUR THICKENING
1 tablespoon cornflour
2 tablespoons water

BLANCHING SOLUTION
1.1 litres (4½ cups) boiling water
1 teaspoon salt
1 teaspoon oil

Remove mushroom stems and soak mushrooms in 750 ml (3 cups) water for 30 minutes. Drain but retain water. Marinate mushrooms for 30 minutes. Rinse and soak dried oysters in 375 ml (1½ cups) water for 30 minutes. Remove grit and rinse oysters thoroughly. Sieve oyster water and retain. Soak sea moss in 375 ml (1½ cups) water for 30 minutes. Remove grit and rinse. Squeeze off excess water and discard water.

Scald roasted trotter in hot water for 2 minutes to remove traces of grease. Rinse and drain.

Heat a claypot till hot, then add in 1 tablespoon oil. When the oil begins to smoke, put in shallot, garlic and ginger and fry till fragrant. Add the marinated mushrooms and fry well for 5 minutes. Now pour in the mushroom and oyster water, cover pot and bring to a boil. Add the scalded trotter and stew for 1 hour over low heat.

Add in the oysters and continue to stew for another 1 hour. If stew is too dry, more hot water can be added.

Wash lettuce and separate leaves. Boil blanching solution and blanch lettuce for 3 minutes. Drain and discard water.

Add in the carrot, sea moss and seasoning. Continue to cook for another 15 minutes. Highlight with 1 teaspoon Chinese rice wine. Check seasoning to suit your taste. If the stew is too thin, thicken with cornflour thickening and stir for 2 minutes before adding blanched lettuce.

冬
菇
燜
雞

○

STEWED CHICKEN WITH MUSHROOMS

2 chicken thighs
4 dried Chinese mushrooms
8 whole shallots, peeled
8 young ginger buds (*chee keong*), skinned
1 clove garlic, bruised and peeled
4 stalks spring onions, cut into 5 cm (2 inch) lengths
900 ml (4½ cups) oil

MARINADE FOR CHICKEN
1 teaspoon salt
1 teaspoon sugar
1 tablespoon ginger juice
1 tablespoon Chinese wine
1 tablespoon cornflour
1 tablespoon oil

SEASONING
½ tablespoon hoisin sauce
150 ml (¾ cups) mushroom water

This is another of my mother's 'stomach-warming' recipes. She said that once the ginger has driven out the 'wind' in the stomach, the stomach would feel more comfortable.

This recipe uses young ginger buds. Ginger buds have a sharp taste and crunchy texture, unlike old ginger which is fibrous and tough.

Trim off mushroom stems and soak mushrooms in 185 ml (¾ cups) warm water for 15 minutes. Squeeze off excess water and retain mushroom water.

Clean and wash chicken thighs. Debone and cut chicken into bite-sized wedges. Marinate for 30 minutes. Bring 1.1 litres (4½ cups) oil to a boil and deep fry marinated chicken for 3 minutes to seal juices. Remove and drain.

Heat 1 tablespoon oil in a claypot till very hot. Fry shallots, ginger buds, garlic and spring onions briskly till fragrant. Then add mushrooms and cook for 5 minutes.

Stir in chicken, reserved mushroom water and seasoning. Cover and cook over high heat for 10 minutes. The gravy should thicken by then.

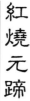

STEWED PORK LOIN

1 pork loin (pig's shoulder)
  about 1.5 kg (3.3 lb)
300 g (10.5 oz) Chinese lettuce
4 star anise
2 stalks spring onions
1 teaspoon salt

4 slices old ginger
1 shallot, sliced
2 teaspoons dark soya sauce
1.5 litres (6 cups) oil
1 teaspoon Chinese rice wine
1 tablespoon oil

STOCK INGREDIENTS
1.5 litres (6 cups) water
200 g (7 oz) chicken bones
100 g (3.5 oz) pork bones

SEASONING A
1 teaspoon salt
2 tablespoons sugar
1 teaspoon light soya sauce

CORNFLOUR THICKENING
½ teaspoon cornflour
1 tablespoon water

SEASONING B
1 tablespoon oyster sauce
1 teaspoon light soya sauce

Certain Western health fads tell us that fats and meat are unhealthy, but according to the principles of Chinese diet, healthy eating means eating everything in moderation.

My mothers insists that gelatinous pig's skin acts as a lubricant and is therefore effective in improving complexion and soothing the intestinal tract.

Health reasons aside, this mouth-watering stew is eaten because it is just too difficult to resist.

Prepare stock by simmering stock ingredients over low flame till the stock is reduced to 600 ml (3 cups). Sieve stock through muslin cloth. Remove hair from pork loin. Rub meat with 1 teaspoon salt. Rinse and drain.

Heat 1 tablespoon oil in a wok. Put in 2 slices of ginger and half of the sliced shallot and fry till fragrant. Pour in 2.3 litres (9 cups) water and bring to a boil.

Add 2 star anises and put in the pork loin. After 10 minutes, lower flame and stew pork loin for 1 hour. Drain and discard stewing liquid. Pat the pork loin dry and coat it evenly with 2 teaspoons dark soya sauce.

Bring 1.5 litres (6 cups) oil to a boil in a wok. Deep fry the pork loin until golden brown (about 10 minutes). Remove, drain and rinse the pork loin.

Heat a saucepan with 1 tablespoon oil until smoky. Sprinkle in 1 teaspoon Chinese rice wine and add in the stock. Include seasoning A, 2 star anises, spring onion and remaining ginger and shallots. Cover lid and bring stock to a boil. Add in the deep-fried pork loin and stew over low heat for 2 hours or until tender. The liquid should be reduced to about ¾ cup.

Wash and dry lettuce and separate the leaves. Arrange of a serving dish.

Place stewed pork loin on the lettuce. Reheat gravy from the stew and add seasoning B. Thicken with cornflour thickening if gravy is too thin. Pour over pork loin and serve.

BRAISED SPICY PORK RIBS

紅燒排骨 ○

Most Chinese recipes use pork ribs for soups and stocks.

Unfortunately, after all the boiling and simmering, the ribs themselves become quite tasteless.

I love spare ribs so this tasty rib stew is one of my favourite dishes. This is specially so as the spices used in the marinade stimulate appetite. This way, I can always eat more!

600 g (1.5 lb) pork spare ribs
2 litres (8 cups) oil
20 g (9.7 oz) garlic, mashed

MARINADE FOR SPARE RIBS
½ teaspoon cornflour
½ teaspoon flour
1 teaspoon salt
1 teaspoon sugar
1 teaspoon five-spice powder
1 tablespoon Chinese rice wine
1 tablespoon satay sauce
1 tablespoon peanut butter
1 tablespoon oil
1 egg

SAUCE
6 tablespoons tomato ketchup
100 g (3.5 oz) palm sugar
2 tablespoons black vinegar
1 teaspoon salt
1 tablespoon lemon juice
450 ml (2¼ cups) hot water

Clean and wash spare ribs. Chop into 10 cm sections and marinate for 1 hour. Heat 1½ litres (9 cups) oil till hot, add in marinated spare ribs and deep fry over medium flame for 5 minutes. Drain. Clean wok.

To make the sauce, reheat the wok with 1 tablespoon oil until smoky and put in garlic and fry till aromatic. Mix all the sauce ingredients and add in the wok. Bring to a boil.

Add the deep-fried spare ribs and mix well. Cover wok and stew spare ribs over low heat until they are moist and well coated with the sauce (about 15 minutes).

Arrange spare ribs on a serving dish, ladle sauce over and serve immediately.

DOUBLE BOILING

滋
補
燉
品

Double boiling: the traditional way of preparing nutritious tonics.

There is a Chinese saying that goes: Medicine and food are derived from one source 医食同源. That is to say, the purpose of eating food and taking medicine is the same – we want to be healthy. However, another saying goes: If medicine is eaten to restore health, it is better to eat nutritious food to fortify the body 药補不如食補.

The traditional way of preparing nutritious tonics in the Chinese kitchen is by double boiling 炖. The character 屯, which appears next to the ideogram for fire 火 means 'classic' or 'elegant'. Thus, double boiling is seen by Chinese cooks as a refined culinary technique which brings out the essence of herbal and other ingredients. Double boiled tonics and foods are believed to, among others, rejuvenate and improve the complexion, restore health, replenish energy and revitalise blood circulation.

Traditionally, double boiling is cooking in a closed container which is heated by placing it in a larger container of boiling water. The water in the outer pot is kept simmering over low to medium heat to provide the constant temperature required to cook the food placed in the inner pot. This process is over a prolonged period of 3-4 hours, but since there is no direct heat used, there is little chance of burning the food. Also, with low evaporation, the food values of the ingredients are completely locked in, giving double boiled soups a stronger and more distinct flavour than boiled soups. Today, double boiling is made even simpler, with the use of a double-boiler, crock pot or pressure cooker.

For successful double boiling, the water level should be no higher than half of the outer pot so that when the water boils, the boiling will not cause the cover of the inner pot to open and spill water into the food. However, care must be taken to maintain the water level and to keep the cooking temperature constant. Have a pot of boiling water at hand and add boiling water into the outer pot when necessary. Although the water is kept on medium to low heat, it must be kept simmering so that the pot of food is properly heated throughout the cooking time. Traditionally, a strip of sandpaper is used to seal the lid of the inner pot to make sure that there is no loss of liquid by evaporation and that the pot of food will not be spilled by the boiling water.

The process of double boiling is made easier with a pot specially designed for the purpose. It consists of a lidded enamel pot with a long handle which sits in another pot for the boiling water. This double-boiler can be easily obtained at Chinese hardware shops.

KITCHENWARE

Large lidded saucepan

Tripod

Broad lidded tureen

Tall lidded tureen

Enamel or porcelain double-boiler

Soup ladle

Colander ladle

Sandpaper

Shallow bamboo basket with strings
tied to its corners

INGREDIENTS SUITABLE FOR DOUBLE BOILING

SEAFOOD	VEGETABLES	MISCELLANEOUS	MEAT
Fish	Chinese cabbage	Shark's fin	Lean pork
Tortoise	Carrot	Snow fungus	Chicken
Turtle	Apples	Snow frog's gland	Black-skinned chicken
Dried scallop	Chinese pear	Bird's nest	Duck
Pearl scallop	Papaya	Rock sugar	Pigeon
Dried abalone	Chinese herbs		Quail
			Frog

TEMPERATURE AND COOKING TIMES

Double-Boiler: 3 to 4 hours at low medium heat

Pressure Cooker: after the whistle then one third of the time required in the
recipe, low to medium heat

Crock Pot: double the regular cooking time at high heat

SEA CUCUMBER & SCALLOP SOUP

瑤柱燉海參 ○

2 sea cucumbers
20 g (0.7 oz) dried scallops
10 g (0.3 oz) dioscorea (*wai san*)
10 g medlar seeds (*kei chee*)
2 slices old ginger
1 teaspoon salt, or to taste
1.5 litres (6 cups) warm water

FOR SCALDING SEA CUCUMBERS
2 slices old ginger
2 stalks spring onions
½ teaspoon Chinese rice wine
Hot water to cover sea cucumbers

Sea cucumber (Stichopus japonicus) is one of the top delicacies of Chinese cuisine. Traditionally, these jelly-like sea slugs are known as the 'ginseng of the sea' 海參 because they have similar properties as ginseng.

Besides being used in stews, sea cucumbers are just as tasty if double boiled with some dried scallops.

This is one of my favourite soups for replenishing 'yang' essence.

Rinse diocsorea and medlar seeds.

Wash and soak scallops in 375 ml (1½ cups) warm water for 1 hour. Drain and retain scallop water.

Pour 1.1 litres (4½ cups) of hot water and scallop water into a double-boiler, add dioscorea and medlar seeds and double boil for 2 hours over medium flame.

Bring scalding liquid for the sea cucumbers to a boil. Put in the sea cucumbers and cook for 10 minutes. Ladle out sea cucumbers and discard the liquid, ginger and spring onions.

Rinse and cut sea cucumbers into thick sections. When the scallop soup has double boiled for 2 hours, add sea cucumbers and ginger.

Continue to double boil for another 1 hour.

Season with salt before serving.

菜
膽
燉
翅

☯

SHARK'S FIN
WITH CHINESE CABBAGE HEARTS

400 g (14 oz) frozen shark's fins
200 g (7 oz) Chinese cabbage hearts (*pak choy tam*)
2 slices Chinese ham (20 g, 0.7 oz) scalded
Red Chinese vinegar for dipping sauce
4 slices ginger

SEASONING
1 teaspoon salt
4 teaspoons Chinese rice wine

FOR SCALDING SHARK'S FINS
2 slices old ginger
2 stalks spring onions
2 teaspoons Chinese rice wine
1.5 litres (6 cups) water
1 teaspoon oil

FOR SUPERIOR STOCK
½ chicken
200 g (7 oz) spare ribs
2 dried scallops
2.3 litres (9 cups) water
1 teaspoon salt

I once asked my father why he added Chinese cabbage hearts when he double boiled shark's fin soup. He said that he did so for two reasons. First, Chinese cabbage hearts are refreshing, and second, being costly, it was a good vegetable to complement such a choice ingredient as shark's fin.

Since shark's fins are high in protein and minerals, they revitalise the major organs, especially the spleen and stomach. The use of the ham and wine in this recipe highlights the subtle flavours of the soup.

Cook the ingredients for superior stock in a pot for 2 hours or until the liquid is reduced to 1.1 litres (4½ cups).

Combine ingredients for scalding shark's fins and bring to a boil. Add in shark's fins and cook for 15 minutes. Drain and discard ginger and spring onions.

Wash and drain Chinese cabbage hearts. Cut ham into matchstick strips.

Divide shark's fins into 4 equal portions and put into individual serving bowls. Fill each bowl ¾ full with superior stock. Sprinkle ham on top, cover lid and double boil over low flame for 2 hours.

Add cabbage hearts and ginger to each bowl and continue to double boil over low flame for another hour.

Season with salt and wine and serve with a little plate of red Chinese vinegar.

合桃燉雞

○

CHICKEN & WALNUT SOUP

1 medium-sized chicken (1.5 kg, 3.3 lb)
100 g (3.5 oz) shelled walnuts
10 g (0.3 oz) dioscorea (*wai san*)
1.9 litres (7½ cups) hot water
1 teaspoon salt

Wash dioscorea and soak in water for 15 minutes. Drain.
   Gut chicken and wash thoroughly. Scald in hot water for 3 minutes.
   Put all ingredients into a double-boiler, add 1¼ litres (7½ cups) of hot water and cover lid. Double boil for 4 hours over low flame.
   Season with salt before serving. Complement the cooked ingredients with a small plate of light soya sauce.

My mother takes good care of her hair and complexion and thus, has always liked having nuts in her soup for their 'lubricating' qualities. In particular, she fancied walnuts, which is a good choice, since walnuts are traditionally favoured as a food which improves blood circulation.

During the dry season, mother double-boiled this nourishing soup for us, saying that because it improves the functions of the spleen, stomach and kidneys, it strengthens the body and promotes good blood circulation.

雪蛤燉雞

☯

CHICKEN & SNOW FROG GLANDS SOUP

1 medium-sized chicken (about 1½ kg, 3.3 lb)
10 g (0.3 oz) snow frog glands (*shuet kap ko*)
8 red dates, stoned and rinsed
1 slice old ginger
1 slice lean Chinese ham OR 2 dried scallops
1.9 litres (7½ cups) hot water
1 teaspoon salt, optional

Snow frog glands have a slight fishy smell. This can be minimised by scalding it in hot water with a couple of slices of ginger. This soup is good for general health.

Soak snow frog's glands in warm water for 4 hours. Remove veins. Drain.
   Bring ½ litre (3 cups) of water to a boil. Add in ginger and soak frog glands. Boil briskly for 5 minutes. Rinse ingredients with cold water and drain. Discard ginger.
   Gut chicken and wash thoroughly. Scald in hot water. Scald ham briefly.
   Put chicken, frog glands and red dates into a double-boiler. Add 1.9 litres (7½ cups) hot water, cover lid and double boil over low flame for 3 hours. Season the soup with salt, if necessary, before serving.

参
鬚
燉
鷄
湯
○

KOREAN GINSENG & CHICKEN SOUP

1 small chicken (1 kg, 2.2 lb)
10 g (0.3 oz) Korean ginseng roots (*ko lai sum so*)
10 g (0.3 oz) dioscorea (*wai san*)
10 g (0.3 oz) medlar seeds (*kei chee*)
10 g (0.3 oz) polyconattum (*yok chok*)
30 g (1 oz) snow fungus (*shuet yee*), soaked
5 g (0.15 oz) dried longan flesh
2.3 litres (9 cups) hot water
1 teaspoon salt, or to taste

As all the herbs used in this recipe promote blood circulation and improve general health, this very light tonic is ideal for those who always feel tired and fatigued. You will be surprised how energetic you feel after a couple of bowls of this soup.

Gut chicken, wash thoroughly and scald in hot water for 3 minutes.

Rinse briefly all herbs, snow fungus and dried longan flesh separately.

Put scalded chicken and all the ingredients into double-boiler. Add 2.3 litres (9 cups) of hot water and cover lid. Double boil over low flame for 4 hours.

Season with salt just before serving. The soup and the cooked ingredients may be served separately. Complement cooked ingredients with a little plate of light soya sauce.

杏
仁
燉
雪
梨
●

CHINESE PEARS WITH ALMONDS

4 Chinese pears
10 g (0.3 oz) sweet and bitter almond mixture
100 g (3.5 oz) rock sugar
1.5 litres (6 cups) hot water

SALT SOLUTION FOR PEARS
500 ml (2 cups) hot water
½ teaspoon salt

Sweet and bitter almonds are kernels from different species of apricot. The smaller bitter almonds have stronger herbal properties and are usually not recommended to be eaten alone. They are, therefore, mixed in the proportion 1:10 with the bigger sweet almonds.

Sweet and bitter almond mixture is available, mixed in the correct proportion, from Chinese medical halls. In this recipe, the pears are double-boiled and chilled as a dessert. A little almond mixture is added to enhance the flavour of the pears. This dessert and its sweet soup are good for alleviating dry coughs.

Wash and cut pears into quarters into big wedges. Core. Skin if preferred. Soak in salt solution for 1 minute. Drain.

Rinse almonds and rock sugar briefly.

Put all ingredients into a double-boiler. Add 1.5 litres (6 cups) of hot water, cover and double boil over low flame for 3 hours. Serve hot or chilled.

VARIATION: *The pears can be skinned and kept whole for a pretty presentation. 4 red apples or 1 medium sized papaya can be used in place of the Chinese pears in this recipe.*

TURTLE SOUP WITH HERBS

500 g (1.1 lb) turtle meat or 1 small turtle
20 g (0.7 oz) dioscorea (*wai san*)
40 g (1.3 oz) Chinese cordyceps (*tong chung choe*)
20 g (0.7 oz) medlar seeds (*kei chee*)
10 g (0.3 oz) sweet and bitter almond mixture (see page 213)
10 g (0.3 oz) dried longan flesh
2.3 litres (9 cups) hot water
2 teaspoons salt

SEASONING
1 teaspoon salt
1 tablespoon Chinese rice wine (optional)

Have the turtle slaughtered and prepared when you buy it from the market. It should be cleaned and gutted, but ask for the offal which is nutritious and used in this recipe. You will also need the shell which should be kept whole.

Discard any remaining fatty tissue found in the cavity of the turtle. Rub the cavity with 1 teaspoon salt and rinse thoroughly. Scald the turtle in hot water for 5 minutes and remove membranes found on the flesh. Rinse thoroughly. Rub offal with 1 teaspoon salt and rinse.

Rinse all the herbs briefly.

Stuff the offal into the turtle and place the turtle in a tureen. Put the shell on the turtle and put the herbs around it. Add 2.3 litres (9 cups) hot water, cover the tureen and double boil over low flame for 3½ hours.

When it is done, add seasoning and serve hot. The cooked ingredients can be served separately with a plate of light soy sauce.

Turtles have great nutritional value, from their shell to the ligaments around their fleshy body.

When I was young, I drank a lot of this soup on the insistence of my father who said that I needed it to fortify my 'yin' essence. I agreed with him, especially after gruelling Chinese opera lessons!

CHICKEN STUFFED WITH POMELO

柚肉燉鷄湯 ◐

1 fresh pomelo
1 medium-sized chicken (1½ kg or 3.3 lbs), cleaned
1 piece preserved tangerine peel
1.5 litres (6 cups) boiling water
1 tablespoon salt

Peel pomelo and separate into segments. Separate the flesh from the rind, discard the seeds and set the flesh aside.

Wash tangerine peel and soak for 15 minutes. Discard water.

Stuff pomelo flesh and tangerine peel into cavity of the chicken and secure the opening with toothpicks.

Put the chicken into a double-boiler, add the boiling water and double boil for 3½ hours over low flame. Add salt before serving in a tureen. Provide light soya sauce as a dipping sauce for the chicken.

Pomelos are as ubiquitous as mooncakes during the Mid-autumn or Lantern Festival which falls on the fifteenth day of the eighth moon.

My family gathers together for a reunion dinner on this night when the moon is said to appear brightest and biggest every year. After the meal, we adjourn to the courtyard to admire and worship the moon. An altar, laden with mooncakes, Chinese tea, flowers and fruits, is set up. Among the fruits offered is always the pomelo which, to the Chinese, symbolises togetherness.

As children, we were not allowed to have too much of the raw fruit because of its 'cooling' and 'damp' qualities. However, a few days after the festival, Grandmother would cook this chicken and pomelo soup for us. This soup strengthens the spleen and stomach and also alleviates coughs and colds caused by the dry season.

SNOW FUNGUS
& PAPAYA DELIGHT

木瓜燉雪耳 ☯

1 ripe papaya (about 1–1.5 kg, 2.2–3.3 lb)
50 g (2 oz) snow fungus
10 g (0.3 oz) sweet and bitter almond mixture (see page 213)
120 g (5 oz) rock sugar
1.5 litres (6 cups) hot water

Soak snow fungus in warm water for an hour. Trim stems and tear fungus into little florets. Rinse briefly under a running tap to remove grit. Drain.

Rinse and cut papaya into two, lengthwise. Remove seeds. Scoop out balls of papaya flesh and set aside. Rinse rock sugar briefly.

Put the snow fungus, almond mixture, rock sugar and 1.5 litres (6 cups) of hot water into a double boiler. Cover and double boil for 2 hours over low flame.

Add the balls of papaya flesh and continue to double boil for another hour. Serve hot or chilled.

Traditionally, the Chinese regard the papaya as a fruit with 'soothing' qualities. The snow fungus and almond mixture strengthen the lungs, and with the addition of rock sugar, this soup is good for moistening the lungs.

This refreshing soup is usually served as a dessert during hot, dry spells.

SNOW FUNGUS SOUP

冰花燉雪耳 ☯

50 g (2 oz) snow fungus (*shuet yee*)
40 g (1.3 oz) lilium brownii (*pak hup*)
10 g sweet and bitter almond mixture (see page 213)
100 g (3.5 oz) rock sugar
1.5 litres (6 cups) hot water

Soak snow fungus in warm water for 1 hour. Trim off stems and tear into pieces. Rinse and drain. Rinse other ingredients briefly.

Put all ingredients, including 1.5 litres (6 cups) of hot water, into a double-boiler; cover lid and double boil for 3 hours. Serve hot or chilled.

This sweet soup is an all-time favourite of my family. The Chinese enjoy the cruchiness of the snow fungus and regard it as one of the most valuable delicacies in their cuisine.

From the Tremellaceae fungus family, snow fungus benefits the lungs, stomach and kidneys. And if you need that extra glow in your complexion, you can also rely on snow fungus to give that effect.

泡參燉鮑甫

ABALONE, CHICKEN & AMERICAN GINSENG SOUP

100 g (3.5 oz) dried abalone slices
1 small chicken (1 kg, 2.2 lb)
20 g (0.7 oz) American wild ginseng (*pao sum*)
2 slices of old ginger
1.9 litres (7½ cups) hot water

SEASONING
1 tablespoon salt
1 tablespoon Chinese rice wine

This is my 'examination tonic'!

My father double boiled this soup for me only when I burnt the midnight oil, mugging for exams.

This soothing tonic is good for renewing tired minds and bodies.

Soak abalone slices in water for 30 minutes.

Gut chicken and wash thoroughly. Scald in hot water for 3 minutes. Rinse.

Put all the ingredients into a double-boiler. Pour in 1.9 litres (7½ cups) hot water, cover and double boil over low flame for 4 hours. Season just before serving in a tureen.

鮑魚燉雞

CHICKEN WITH ABALONE SOUP

1 medium-sized chicken (1.5 kg, 3.3 lb)
6 slices dried abalone
1.9 litres (7½ cups) hot water
1 teaspoon salt

Rinse abalone slices briefly.

Gut and wash chicken thoroughly. Scald chicken in hot water for 3 minutes.

Put all the ingredients into a double-boiler, add 1.9 litres (7½ cups) hot water and cover lid. Double boil over low flame for 3 hours.

Season with salt before serving. Serve hot.

冬菇燉雞湯 ◐

CHINESE MUSHROOM WITH CHICKEN SOUP

1 medium-sized chicken (1.5 kg, 3.3 lb)

8 dried mushrooms

1 carrot

1 slice old ginger

1.5 litres (6 cups) hot water

1 teaspoon salt

Trim off mushroom stems. Soak mushrooms in 300 ml (1½ cups) warm water for 30 minutes. Squeeze out excess water. Retain water for later use.

Gut chicken and wash thoroughly. Scald chicken in hot water for 3 minutes.

Skin carrot and cut carrot into thick slices.

Put all the ingredients, except salt, into a double-boiler, add 1.5 litres (6 cups) of hot water and the reserved mushroom water. Cover lid and double boil over low flame for 3 hours.

Season with salt before serving. Serve hot.

If you have the impression that all Chinese nutritious soups must contain herbs, this recipe will remove the misconception.

The rich soup is golden and delicious, with the nutrition coming from the tasty dried mushrooms and the sweet carrots.

Your children are sure to love it.

栗米鬚燉橫利 ●

PIG'S SPLEEN WITH CORN SILK

40 g (1.3 oz) corn silk (*suk mai so*)

1 pig's spleen

200 g (7 oz) shin pork

30 g (1 oz) dioscorea (*wai san*)

1.5 litres (6 cups) hot water

1 teaspoon salt

Wash and drain corn silk. Wash and clean spleen. Remove fat.

Scald pig's spleen and shin pork in hot water for 3 minutes.

Put all ingredients into a double-boiler. Pour in 1.5 litres (6 cups) of hot water, cover lid and double boil over low flame for 3 hours.

Add the teaspoon of salt before serving. Serve hot.

The corn silk used in this recipe are the golden-brown thread-like growths on the top of young corn.

Together with dioscorea and pig's spleen, this tonic, although not a cure, is beneficial to diabetics.

冬
瓜
鴨
腎
湯
☯

WINTER MELON
& DUCK GIZZARD SOUP

600 g (1.3 oz) winter melon, skinned and diced
1 dried duck gizzard, diced
2 fresh duck gizzard, diced
80 g (2.8 oz) carrot, skinned and diced
4 Chinese mushrooms, soaked and diced
10 g (0.3 oz) medlar seeds (*kei chee*)
10 g (0.3 oz) dried longan flesh
80 g (2.8 oz) lotus seeds
10 g (0.3 oz) snow fungus (*shuet yee*)
5 g (0.15 oz) white peppercorns
1 teaspoon salt

FOR SUPERIOR STOCK
300 g (10.6 oz) lean meat
½ chicken
10 g (0.3 oz) Chinese ham
3.8 litres (15 cups) hot water

If you doubt the ancient Chinese concept of balancing 'yin' and 'yang' ingredients into harmonious and nutritious foods, try this recipe. It is one of my masterpieces based on the 'yin-yang' concept for the hot season.

Fresh and dried duck gizzards, able to disperse heaty elements, flavour the bland winter melon which possesses 'yin' characteristics. This is matched by dried longan flesh which has 'yang' elements, and the lotus seeds which is 'neutral'. Slowly cooked in a double-boiler, all the goodness of the ingredients are distilled and combined into a clear, golden soup.

If you still have doubts or still cannot fathom the concept about 'heaty', 'cooling' and 'neutral' foods, just take my mother's advice: "Drink it, it's good for you!"

Prepare superior stock by simmering all the stock ingredients for 3 hours over low heat. Sieve stock through a muslin cloth.

Soak snow fungus in water for 1 hour. Remove grit and tear fungus into florets. Boil lotus seeds in water for 30 minutes. Rinse and remove skin. Drain.

Rinse medlar seeds and longan flesh briefly.

Put diced gizzards, carrots, mushrooms, herbs, peppercorns and lotus seeds into a double-boiler. Pour in 2.3 litres (9 cups) superior stock. Cover lid and double boil over medium flame for 2 hours.

Add the diced winter melon and snow fungus and continue to double boil for another 1 hour. Check seasoning and add a teaspoon of salt, if your prefer, before serving.

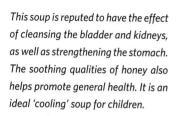

My nanny cooked this soup for me and now, in turn, I cook it for my children. This sweet soup is a popular Chinese snack which strengthens the stomach and kidneys.

白果燉茨實 ◖

GINGKO WITH FEROX NUT SOUP

200 g (7 oz) gingko nuts
50 g (2 oz) ferox nuts (*see sut*)
8 red dates (*hung choe*), stoned
20 g (0.7 oz) dried longan flesh
80 g (2.8 oz) rock sugar
2.3 litres (9 cups) hot water

Shell gingko nuts and remove membranes. Rinse ferox nuts, red dates and dried longan flesh.

Put all ingredients into a double-boiler with 2.3 litres (9 cups) hot water. Cover lid and double boil over medium flame for 3 hours. Serve hot.

蜜汁茨實 ●

FEROX NUT & HONEY SOUP

50 g (2 oz) ferox nuts (*see sut*)
6 red dates, stoned and rinsed
150 ml (¾ cup) honey
50 g (2 oz) rock sugar
2.3 litres (9 cups) hot water

Wash ferox nuts and soak in warm water for an hour. Drain.

Put soaked ferox nuts and 2.3 litres (9 cups) of hot water in a saucepan. Add red dates, cover lid and cook over low flame for 2 hours.

Add honey and rock sugar and continue to cook over low flame for another hour. Serve hot or chilled.

FOR CROCK-POT USERS: *Use 1.3 litres (5 cups) hot water and cook at high for 3 hours. Then add honey and rock sugar and continue cooking at high for another 3 hours.*

This soup is reputed to have the effect of cleansing the bladder and kidneys, as well as strengthening the stomach. The soothing qualities of honey also helps promote general health. It is an ideal 'cooling' soup for children.

燉
羊
肉
○

HERBAL MUTTON SOUP

500 g (1.1 lb) mutton
80 g (2.8 oz) black beans (hak dao)
20 g (0.7 oz) sliced anglelica (tong kwai)
10 g (0.3 oz) dried longan flesh
1.9 litres (7½ cups) hot water
1 teaspoon salt

Anglelica or tong kwai is known to possess properties which improve blood circulation. This is why the old folks of my family have this tonic from time to time to fortify their system.

Trim excess fat from mutton. Scald mutton in hot water for 2 minutes. Rinse and discard water. Wash herbs briefly.

Put all ingredients, except salt, into a double-boiler and add in 1.9 litres (7½ cups) hot water. Cover lid and double boil over medium flame for 3½ hours.

Season with salt before serving. Serve hot. Complement mutton with a small plate of light soy sauce.

高
麗
參
燉
鷄
○

CHICKEN & GINSENG SOUP

1 small chicken (1 kg, 2.2 lb)
5-8 slices Korean ginseng (ko lai sum)
½ tablespoon Chinese rice wine
1 teaspoon salt, optional
1.5 litres (6 cups) hot water

Ginseng (Panax ginseng C.A. May) is found in China's Jilin province and Korea. The character 人 in its Chinese name 人參 means 'person', alluding to the fact that some ginseng roots look like human figures with arms, legs and head. After the harvest, raw ginseng roots are seasoned and dried in the sun to give them their brownish-red colouring. Ginseng has long been regarded as a universal panacea, possessing dual properties; in itself, it can either be energy-giving and have healing properties or act as a sedative. The old folks at home used to have this soup to strengthen their overall vitality. It is best drunk before bedtime.

Gut chicken and wash thoroughly. Rub with salt and rinse well. Scald chicken in hot water for 3 minutes. Drain.

Stuff half the amount of ginseng into the cavity of the chicken. Seal opening with toothpicks.

Put the stuffed chicken into a double-boiler and add the remaining ginseng slices.

Pour in 1.5 litres (6 cups) of hot water. Cover lid and double boil over medium flame for 4 hours.

Add Chinese rice wine and also salt, if required, just before serving. Serve hot.

泡
參
燉
鮑
甫
☯

BIRD'S NEST SOUP

40 g (1.3 oz) bird's nest
50 g (2 oz) rock sugar
6 honey dates (*mut choe*)
10 g (0.3 oz) American wild ginseng (*pao sum*)
10 g (0.3 oz) sweet and bitter almond mixture (see page 213)
1.5 litres (6 cups) hot water

Soak bird's nest in warm water for 1 hour. Remove impurities and drain.
Put soaked bird's nest and all other ingredients into a double-boiler. Add 1.5 litres (5 cups) of hot water. Cover lid and double boil over low flame for 3 hours. Serve hot or chilled.

Many of my students shrink at the idea of eating a nest made of birds' vomit. In response, I tell them that if they accept the nutritional value of honey, then they should also have confidence in bird's vomit. After all, is there a difference between birds and bees in this context?

Bird's nest is produced by swallows (Collocal esculenta) *found in the coastal regions of South-east China and South-east Asia. Feeding on seafood and plankton, the birds regurgitate a sticky, jelly-like substance with which they make their nests on cliff walls and deep coastal caves.*

The risk involved in collecting these nests make bird's nests one of the most costly ingredients in Chinese cuisine. Is it a wonder then that in ancient times, only royalty and the very rich could enjoy this noble food.

Though my mother is the one who is against using expensive ingredients, she accepts that nothing can quite replace bird's nest. After all, if it can restore youth and improve complexion, who cares about price!

花膠燉乳鴿 ☯

PIGEON WITH FISH MAW

This was my grandmother's favourite tonic. She said that pigeon can 'warm' the body better than chicken, revitalising the 'chi' or circulatory system.

My research revealed that fish maw replenishes the 'yin' essence and is also good for the complexion. This is a 'neutral' soup.

2 pigeons, 500 g (1 lb) each
100 g (3.5 oz) lean pork
50 g (2 oz) dried fish maw, soaked
20 g (0.7 oz) Chinese ham
1 slice old ginger
1 teaspoon Chinese rice wine
1.5 litres (6 cups) hot water

FOR SCALDING FISH MAW
1 stalk spring onions
1 slice old ginger
1 tablespoon Chinese rice wine
1 teaspoon oil
750 ml (3 cups) water

SEASONING
1 teaspoon salt
1 teaspoon Chinese rice wine

Clean, gut and wash pigeons.

Scald lean pork and pigeons in hot water for 3 minutes.

Place pork and pigeons inside double-boiler. Add in ginger, ham and 1.5 litres (6 cups) of hot water. Cover lid and double boil over low flame for 3 hours.

Meanwhile, soak fish maw for 1 hour. Drain.

Bring scalding mixture for fish maw to a boil. Add in soaked fish maw and cook for 5 minutes. Drain and discard spring onions and ginger.

After pork and pigeons have been cooked for 3 hours, add the prepared fish maw and continue to double boil the mixture over low flame for another 45 minutes.

Season with salt and wine. Serve this dish hot, with a little plate of soya sauce as a dipping sauce.

VARIATION: *If pigeons are unavailable, substitute with black chickens.*

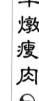

CORDYCEPS SOUP

40 g (1.3 oz) Chinese cordyceps *(tong chong choe)*
10 g (0.3 oz) dioscorea *(wai san)*
10 g (0.3 oz) medlar seeds *(kei chee)*
5 g (0.15 oz) dried longan flesh
1.5 litres (6 cups) hot water
1 teaspoon salt

CHOICE OF MEAT
200 g (7 oz) lean pork
OR 1 chicken (1 kg, 2.2 lb)
OR 1 duck (1½ kg, 3.3lb)

Wash and clean meat thoroughly. Scald in hot water for 3 minutes.

Untie cordyceps and rinse all herbs and dried longan flesh briefly.

Put ingredients and meat into a double-boiler, add 1.5 litres (6 cups) of hot water, cover lid and double boil over low flame for 4 hours.

Season with salt just before serving. The soup and the cooked ingredients may be served separately. Complement cooked ingredients with a little plate of light soya sauce.

Chinese cordyceps have a fascinating life-cycle. According to Chinese botanical records, the cordycep is a combination of plant and animal matter.

The brown tuber-like parts of cordyceps were originally worms which lived underground. These worms were covered with spores which, in turn, nurtured another minute larvae. During winter, the spores and larvae draw nutrition from their hosts and by summer, the worms are left shrivelled up while the spores send shoots upward from the heads of their hosts. These shoots are the black thread-like parts of cordyceps.

The Chinese name for this costly herb attempts to summarise this unusual metamorphosis. It is known as 冬虫夏草 or 'winter worm and summer grass'.

I highly recommend this tonic for strengthening kidneys and restoring general health.

PIG'S BRAIN & CHICKEN FEET SOUP

歡天喜地湯 ○

2 sets pig's brain
4 chicken feet
10 g (0.3 oz) dioscorea (*wai san*)
10 g (0.3 oz) medlar seeds (*kei chee*)
5 g dried longan flesh
1 slice old ginger, optional
1.5 litres (6 cups) hot water
1 teaspoon salt, or to taste

Soak pig's brains in water. Remove membrane and veins. Scald in hot water for 1 minute. Drain and set aside.

Wash chicken feet and cut off claws. Scald for a minute in hot water.

Rinse herbs and longan flesh briefly.

Put chicken feet, herbs, longan flesh and ginger into a double-boiler, add 1.5 litres (6 cups) of hot water and cover lid. Double boil for 3 hours over low flame.

Now include the scalded pig's brain and continue to double boil for another 1 hour.

Add salt and serve soup and cooked ingredients hot. Complement cooked ingredients with a small plate of light soya sauce.

The Chinese eat every part of every creature, the concept being the eating of a particular part of an animal will benefit the corresponding part of the eater 食形補形. This recipe is a good example of that concept.

My father was rather impatient and he liked quick and accurate work in his kitchen. He could not tolerate forgetful or slow kitchen hands and I was not given special treatment.

Fortunately, our restaurant served this soup daily and I always had a bowl whenever I needed to nourish the brain and strengthen my leg muscles for the mental energy and quick reflexes required for working in my father's kitchen.

Appropriately, this soup was listed in our menu as 欢天喜地汤 Happy Heavens and Joyous Earth Soup, implying that those who drank it would be delighted from head to toe.

牛尾湯

CHINESE OXTAIL SOUP

500 g (1.1 lb) ox-tails, cut into big sections
20 g (0.7 oz) dioscorea (wai san)
20 g (0.7 oz) medlar seeds (kei chee)
10 g (0.3 oz) dried longan flesh
2.3 litres (9 cups) hot water
1 teaspoon salt

Wash ox-tails and scald in hot water for 3 minutes. Rinse. Wash all herbs briefly.

Put all ingredients, except salt, in a double-boiler and add in 2.3 litres (9 cups) hot water. Cover lid and double boil over medium flame for 4 hours.

Season with salt and serve soup hot. Complement cooked ingredients with a plate of light soya sauce.

Chinese folk believe that beef possesses 'heaty' elements and should, therefore, be eaten sparingly. My father who loved beef, agreed and said that, when eaten moderately, it could strengthen blood circulation.

The gelatinous tendons of ox-tail gently double boiled with choice herbs produce a rich and delicious soup.

燉珍珠肉 ●

PEARL SCALLOP SOUP

40 g (1.3 oz) dried pearl scallops (*chun chue yok*)
300g (10.5 oz) shin pork
10 g (0.3 oz) medlar seeds (*kei chee*)
10 g (0.3 oz) dioscorea (*wai san*)
2 slices old ginger
1.5 litres (6 cups) hot water
1 teaspoon salt

Wash and drain pearl scallop.

Scald pork in hot water for 3 minutes. Rinse and drain.

Rinse medlar seeds and dioscorea briefly.

Put ingredients, including ginger, into a double-boiler. Add 1.5 litres (6 cups) of hot water, cover lid and double boil over low flame for 3 hours.

Season with salt before serving.

It was my father who first taught me to appreciate dried pearl scallops. His opinion was that dried pearl scallops are far superior in taste than ordinary dried scallops.

Besides this, dried pearl scallops have a very distinctive flavour which is not found in other dried seafoods. It is also one of the choice ingredients for replenishing 'yin' essence.

Available from Chinese dried goods stores, they are highly prized and, as its name indicates, is as valuable as pearls.

黑豆燉豬蹄 ○

PIG'S TROTTER & BLACK BEAN SOUP

1 pig's trotter (foreleg), cut into sections
50 g (2 oz) black beans (hak dao), fried without oil
6 red dates, stoned
100 (3.5 oz) old ginger root, washed and crushed
20 g (0.7 oz) eucommia (tu chung)
1.1 litres (4½ cups) hot water
1 teaspoon salt

Clean and wash pig's trotter. Pluck hairs. Scald trotters in hot water for 3 minutes. Rinse.

Put all ingredients, including the 1.1 litres (4½ cups) hot water, into a double-boiler. Cover lid and double boil over low flame for 4 hours.

Pour soup into a tureen and serve hot. Discard eucommia – it is not eaten as it is bitter – and serve remaining cooked ingredients separately with a little plate of light soya sauce.

Tu chung, botanically known as Eucommia ulmoides olio, is the bark of a tree found mainly in Sichuan, Hubei and Henan. They are prized by the Chinese as a herb which relieves backaches and strengthens the kidneys.

The older folk in my family have this soup once a month as it is good for strengthening the lumbar bones and improving blood circulation.

紅棗燉雪蛤 ☯

DOUBLE-BOILED SNOW FROG GLANDS

10 g (0.3 oz) snow frog glands (shuet kap ko)
50 g (2 oz) rock sugar
20 g (0.7 oz) dried longan flesh
8 red dates, stoned and rinsed
1 small stalk pandanus leaf, optional
1.5 litres (6 cups) hot water

Devein frog glands, then soak in warm water for 4 hours. Drain.

Scald soaked frog glands in hot water for 3 minutes. Drain.

Rinse rock sugar and dried longan flesh briefly before use. Knot pandanus leaves.

Put all the ingredients into a double-boiler. Add the 1.5 litres (6 cups) of hot water, cover lid and double boil over low flame for 3½ hours. Serve hot.

Don't jump at the mention of eating snow frog glands!

This breed of frogs from the north-eastern parts of China is famed for the nutritious fatty glands found in its female. The layer of fatty glands, helps the frogs survive their hibernation through the long, icy winters.

The frogs are caught in the spring and the fatty glands are dried. These brown and knotty dried glands only became light, jelly-like gobs when they are soaked in water. High in nutritional value, snow frog glands are slightly fishy. The smell can be best removed by scalding the glands in hot water with ginger slices.

Double boiled as a sweet soup, snow frog glands is a classic dessert at formal banquets. It is beneficial to those who have weak kidneys and weak knee joints.

PIG'S HEART HERBAL SOUP

燉猪心 ○

Pig's heart, according to Chinese health-food practices, can strengthen the heart, while a few slices of Anglelica (tong kwai) and some black beans are used here to improve blood circulation.

This tonic is therefore useful for those who have weak hearts and have heart palpitations.

1 pig's heart
6 dried mushrooms
20 g (0.7 oz) sliced anglelica (tong kwai)
30 g (1 oz) black beans (hak dao), fried without oil
1 slice of old ginger
2 cloves garlic, crushed with skin
1.5 litres (6 cups) hot water
1 teaspoon salt

Slit pig's heart into two and wash thoroughly. Scald in hot water for 5 minutes. Rinse and drain.

Soak mushrooms for 30 minutes. Squeeze off excess water. Trim stems.

Put all ingredients inside a double-boiler. Add 1.5 litres (6 cups) of hot water, cover lid and double boil over low flame for 4 hours.

Add salt before serving.

CHICKEN & BIRD'S NEST SOUP

鳳吞燕 ☯

If you want to impress your guests with a soup fit for royalty, try this recipe. Traditionally, the rib cage of the chicken is removed and the cavity is stuffed with the bird's nest. This will not fail to impress your guests because of the skill involved in deboning the chicken and the expensive bird's nest required to stuff the bird.

This light, clear and delicious soup is good for restoring general health and improving vitality.

1 medium-sized chicken (1.5 kg, 3.3 lb)
40 g (1.3 oz) bird's nest
2.3 litres (9 cups) hot water
1 teaspoon salt

Clean and gut chicken. Wash thoroughly and drain. Soak bird's nest in 3 bowls of warm water for 2 hours. Remove impurities and drain.

Put the chicken and bird's nest in a double-boiler. The bird's nests can also be stuffed in the cavity of the chicken. Add the 2.3 litres (9 cups) hot water, cover and double boil over low flame for 3 hours.

Season with salt before serving. Serve soup with bird's nest. Serve chicken separately with a small plate of light soya sauce.

雪耳燉瘦肉 ☯

PORK & SNOW FUNGUS SOUP

10 g (0.3 oz) snow fungus (*shuet yee*)
200 g (7 oz) shin pork
30 g (1 oz) lilium brownii (*pak hup*)
4 honey dates (*mut choe*)
10 g (0.3 oz) sweet and bitter almond mixture (see page 213)
1.9 litres (7½ cups) hot water
1 teaspoon salt, optional

Dry coughs in the morning indicate that your lungs 'lack moisture'.

This soup is ideal for those with this condition since the combination of snow fungus, lilium brownii (pak hup) and the almond mixture removes internal heat and 'moistens' the lungs.

Soak snow fungus for 1 hour. Trim off stems and tear fungus into florets.

Scald the shin pork in hot water for 3 minutes. Rinse.

Put all the ingredients into a double-boiler. Pour in 1.9 litres (7½ cups) of hot water, cover lid and double boil over low flame for 3 hours.

When ready, add 1 teaspoon salt if required. Serve hot.

蘋果燉生魚 ☯

SNAKEHEAD FISH & APPLE SOUP

2 red apples
1 snakehead fish (*sang yu*), about 600 g or 1.3 lb
150 g (5.3 oz) lean meat
4 red dates, stoned and rinsed
1 piece preserved tangerine peel
1.5 litres (6 cups) hot water
1 teaspoon salt (optional)

The snakehead, as its name clearly implies, is a fresh water fish which head looks like that of a snake. They are known by the Chinese as 生鱼 *or 'live fish', since they are capable of surviving out of water for some time.*

The flesh of this fish is white, smooth yet firm. Some traditional folk will only buy the fish live since they say that the flesh of the dead fish rapidly loses its firm texture. This is why the fish should be cooked as soon as possible after it is prepared.

My mother cooked this soup for us when we were recovering from illness. It is good for 'soothing' the lungs.

Cut apples into halves and core. Soak apples in a little salt water for 5 minutes. Drain.

Clean and scale snakehead fish. Drain. Scald fish and lean meat separately in hot water for 2 minutes. Rinse and drain.

Rinse tangerine peel briefly.

Put all the ingredients into double-boiler and add in the 1.5 litres (6 cups) hot water. Cover and double boil over low flame for 3 hours.

Season with salt, if necessary, before serving.

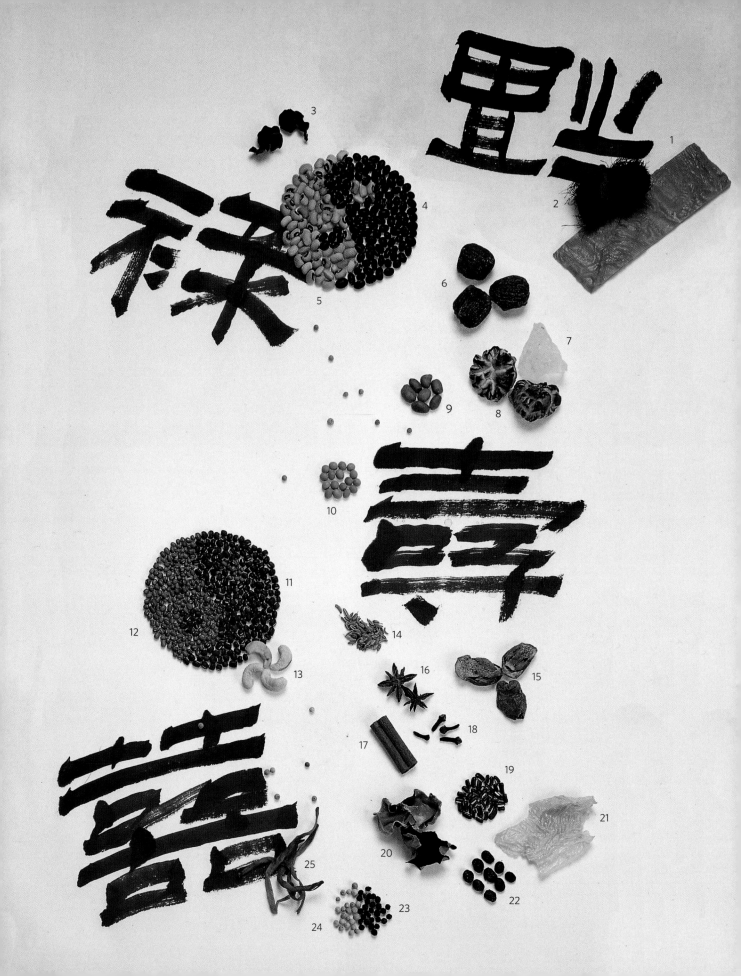

DRIED GOODS

1. Dried sweet beancurd strips
2. Sea moss
3. Cloud fungus
4. Black beans
5. Brow beans
6. Honey dates
7. Rock sugar
8. Dried Chinese mushrooms
9. Raw peanuts
10. Soya beans
11. Red beans
12. Mung beans
13. Cashew nuts
14. Fennel seeds
15. Dried straw mushrooms
16. Star anise
17. Cinnamon
18. Cloves
19. Gram beans
20. Wood fungus
21. Beancurd sheet
22. Fermented black beans
23. Black pepper corns
24. White pepper corns
25. Dried lily buds

NUTRITIONAL
& HERBAL INGREDIENTS

1. Lilium brownii (pak hup)
2. Sweet and bitter almond mixture
3. Dioscorea (wai san)
4. Lotus seeds
5. Cordyceps
6. Snow frog's glands
7. Preserved tangerine peel
8. Red dates
9. Medlar seeds (kei chee)
10. Snow fungus
11. Poria cocos (fook lin)
12. Polyconattum (yok chok)
13. Ferox nuts (see sut)
14. Liquorice (kum choe)
15. Astragalus (puk kay)
16. Barley
17. Walnuts
18. Gingko nuts
19. American wild ginseng
20. Korean ginseng
21. Korean ginseng root
22. Dried longan flesh
23. Dried longan
24. Corn silk
25. Eucommia (tu chung)
26. Buddha's fruit
27. Anglelica (tong kwai)
28. Bird's nests

PROCESSED SEAFOOD

1. Fish maw
2. Fried fish maw
3. Dried pearl scallop
4. Dried oysters
5. Dried shrimps
6. Dried scallops
7. Processed comb shark's fins
8. Dried octopus
9. Dried whole abalone
10. Dried mussels
11. Dried sliced abalone
12. Dried sea cucumber

DRIED GOODS

Brow beans	*mei dao*	Méi Dòu	眉豆
Cashew nuts	*yiew guo*	Yāo Gǔo	腰果
Century eggs	*pei tan*	Pí Dàn	皮蛋
Chinese ham	*for tui*	Húo Tǔi	火腿
Chinese salted eggs	*hum tan*	Xián Dàn	咸蛋
Chinese waxed bacon	*larp yok*	Là Ròu	腊肉
Chinese waxed sausage	*larp cheong*	Là Cháng	腊肠
Chinese waxed liver sausage	*yuen cheong*	Rùn Cháng	胭肠
Chinese wine	*siew zao*	Bái Mǐ Jiǔ	白米酒
Cloud fungus	*wan yee*	Yún Ěr	云耳
Dried beancurd sheet	*fu pei*	Fǔ Pí	腐皮
Dried beancurd strips	*fu chok*	Fǔ Zhù	腐竹
Dried sweet beancurd strips	*fu chok*	Tián Zhù	甜竹
Dried Chinese mushrooms	*ong koo*	Dōng Gū	冬菇
Dried lily buds	*kum chum*	Jīn Zhēn	金针
Dried straw mushrooms	*choe koo*	Cǎo Gū	草菇
Fermented black beans	*dao si*	Dòu Chǐ	豆豉
Flat rice noodles	*sar hor fun*	Shā Hé Fěn	沙河粉
Gram beans	*chaik siew dao*	Chì Xiǎo Dòu	赤小豆
Honey dates	*mut choe*	Mǐ Zhǎo	蜜枣
Hot broad bean paste	*tau ban cheong*	Dòu Bàn Jiàng	豆瓣酱
Kumhua ham	*Kumhua for tui*	Jīn Huá Húo Tǔi	金华火腿
Mung beans	*luk dao*	Lù Dòu	绿豆
Mungbean vermicelli	*fun see*	Fěn Sī	粉丝
Raw peanuts	*fa sang mai*	Huā Shēng Mǐ	花生米
Red beans	*hong dao*	Hóng Dòu	红豆
Red fermented beancurd	*nam yu*	Nán Rǔ	南乳
Rice vermicelli	*mai fun*	Mǐ Fěn	米粉
Rock sugar	*peng tong*	Bīng Táng	冰糖
Sea moss	*fatt choy*	Fà Cài	发菜
Soya beans	*wong dao*	Huáng Dòu	黄豆
Wood fungus	*mok yee*	Mù Ěr	木耳
Yunnan ham	*Wunnam for tui*	Yún Nán Húo Tǔi	云南火腿

HERBS & NUTRITIOUS INGREDIENTS

Almonds (bitter)	Prunus armenica L var ansu Maxim	*pak hung*	Běi Xìng	北杏
Almonds (sweet)	Prunus L.	*lam hung*	Nán Xìng	南杏
American wild ginseng	Panax quinquefolium L.	*pao sum*	Pǎo Shēn	泡参
Anglelica	Anglelica Sinensis (oliv.) Diels.	*tong kwai*	Dǎng Guī	当归
Astragalus	Astragalus membranaceus Bge.	*puk kay*	Bèi Qí	北芪
Black beans	Gycinesoja Sieb et Zucc	*hak dao*	Hēi Dòu	黑豆
Bird's nest	Collocalia esculenta	*yeen wor*	Yàn Wō	燕窝
Buddha's fruit	Momordica grosvenori Swingle	*lor hon kuo*	Luó Hàn Guǒ	罗汉果
Chinese cordyceps	Cordyceps sinensis (Berk.) Sacc	*tong chong choe*	Dōng Chóng Cǎo	冬虫草
Dioscorea	Dioscorea batatas Decne.	*wai san*	Huái Shān	淮山
Dried Longan Flesh	Euphoria longan (Lour.) Steud	*longan yok*	Yuán Ròu	龙眼肉(元肉)
Eucommia	Eucommia Ulmoides Olio	*tu chung*	Dù Zhòng	杜仲
Ferox nuts	Euryale ferox Salisb.	*see sut*	Cì Shí	茨实
Korean ginseng	Panax ginseng C.A. Mey	*ko lai sum*	Gāo Lì Shēn	高丽参
Lilium brownii	Lilium brownii F.E. Brown var. colchesteri wils.	*pak hup*	Bái Hè	百合
Liquorice	Glycyrrhiza uralensis Fisch.	*kum choe*	Gān Cǎo	甘草
Lotus seeds	Nelumbo nucifera Gaertn	*leen chee*	Lián Zi	莲子
Medlar seeds	Lycium chinense Mill	*kei chee*	Qí Zi	杞子
Polyconattum	Polyconattum officinale All	*yok chok*	Yù Zhú	玉竹
Poria cocos	Poria cocos (Schw.) Wolf	*fook lin*	Fù Líng	茯苓
Preserved tangerine peel	Citrus reticulata Blanco	*chan pei*	Chén Pí	陈皮
Red dates	Zizyphus jjuba Mill	*hung choe*	Hóng Zào	红枣
Snow fungus	Tremella fucilormis Berk.	*shuet yee*	Xué Ěr	雪耳
Snow frog's glands	North-eastern China species	*shuet kap ko*	Xué Gé Gāo	雪蛤膏

VEGETABLES & FRUITS

Angled luffa	*see kwa*	Sī Guā	丝瓜
Baby corn	*suk mai sum*	Shú Mǐ Xīn	粟米心
Bamboo shoots	*chok soon*	Zhù Sǔn	竹笋
Beansprouts	*nga choy*	Yá Cài	芽菜
Bittergourd	*fu kwa*	Kǔ Guā	苦瓜
Blanched Chinese chives	*gau wong*	Jiǔ Huáng	韭黄
Broccoli	*kai lan fa*	Sì Lán Hūa	四兰花
Button mushrooms	*mo koo*	Mó Gū	蘑菇
Carrot	*hong lor bak*	Hú Luó Bò	胡罗蔔
Cauliflower	*yeh choy fa*	Yè Cài Huā	椰菜花
Celery	*sai kan*	Sì Qín	四芹
Chinese cabbage	*pak choy*	Bái Cài	白菜
Chinese cabbage hearts	*pak choy tam*	Bái Cài Dǎn	白菜胆
Chinese chive buds	*gau choy fa*	Jiǔ Cài Huā	韭菜花
Chinese lettuce	*sang choy*	Shēng Cài	生菜
Chinese pears	*shuet lei*	Xuè Lì	雪梨
Chinese spinach	*yen choy*	Xián Cài	苋菜
Coriander leaves	*yun sai*	Yán Xī	芫茜
Crystallised Chinese figs	*mo fa kuo*	Wú Huā Guǒ	无花果
Cucumber	*wong kwa*	Huáng Guā	黄瓜
French beans	*sei kwai dao*	Sì Jì Dòu	四季豆
Fresh chestnuts	*luet chee*	Sù Zi	粟子
Garlic	*shun tau*	Suàn Tóu	蒜头
Golden mushrooms	*kum koo*	Jīn Gū	金菇
Green pepper (capsicum)	*chang lat jiew*	Dēng Lóng Jiao	青辣椒
Hairy marrow	*chit kwa*	Jié Guā	节瓜
Iceburg lettuce	*bo lei sang choy*	Bō Lí Shēng Cài	玻璃生菜
Kale	*kai lan*	Gài Lán	芥兰
Kudzu Root	*fun kort*	Fěn Gé	粉葛
Leaf mustard	*kai choy*	Jie Cài	芥菜
Long beans	*dao kort*	Dòu Jiǎo	豆角
Lotus leaves	*leen yeep*	Lián Yè	莲叶
Lotus root	*leen ngau*	Lián Ǒu	莲藕

Mini Chinese cabbage	*siew pak choy*	Xiǎo Bái Cài	小白菜
Mustard greens	*choy sum*	Cài Xīn	菜心
Old cucumber	*lo wong kwa*	Laŏ Huáng Guā	老黄瓜
Old ginger root	*lo keong*	Jiāng	姜
Pandamus Leaf	*pa lang yeep*	Xiāng Lán Yè	香兰叶
Papaya	*mok kwa*	Mù Guā	木瓜
Pea shoots	*dao miew*	Dòu Miáo	豆苗
Pearly beans	*chun chue dao*	Zhēn Zhū Dòu	珍珠豆
Pickled mustard	*jar choy*	Zhà Cài	榨菜
Pineapple	*wong lai/por lor*	Fèng Lí	凤梨
Pomelo	*lok yao*	Yóu Zi	柚子
Red apples	*hong peng kuo*	Hóng Píng Guǒ	红苹果
Red chilli	*hong lart jiew*	Hóng Là Jiāo	红辣椒
Salted preserved mustard	*hum choy*	Xián Cài	咸菜
Shallots	*chong tao jai*	Xiǎo Yáng Cōng	小洋葱
Soft beancurd	*dao fu*	Dòu Fǔ	豆腐
Snow peas	*shuet dao*	Xuè Dòu	雪豆
Soya bean cake	*dao korn*	Dòu Fù Gān	豆腐干
Soya beansprouts	*tai dao gar choy*	Dà Dòu Yá Cài	大豆芽菜
Spanish onions	*yeung chong*	Dà Yáng Cōng	大洋葱
Spring onions	*chong*	Cōng	葱
Sweet potatoes	*farn shue*	Fān Shú	蕃薯
Tientsin cabbage	*wong nga bak (siew choy)*	Huáng Yá Bái	黄牙白
Water chestnuts	*ma tai*	Mǎ Tí	马蹄
Watercress	*sai yong choy*	Xī Yáng Cài	西洋菜
Winter melon	*tung kwa*	Dōng Guā	冬瓜
Young ginger roots	*chee keong*	Zi Jiāng	子姜

PRESERVED SEAFOOD

Canned abalone	*kun tau pao yu*	Guàn Tóu Baò Yú	罐头鲍鱼
Dried abalone	*kon pao yu*	Gān Baò Yú	干鲍鱼
Dried abalone slices	*kon pao yu pin*	Gān Baò Yú Piàn	干鲍鱼片
Dried fish maw	*yu tou*	Yú Dù	鱼肚
Dried mussels	*tum choy*	Dàn Cài	淡菜
Dried oysters	*hou see*	Haó Chǐ	蚝豉
Dried pearl scallops	*chun chue yok*	Zhēn Zhū Ròu	珍珠肉
Dried scallops	*kong yu chee*	Gān Pèi	干贝（江瑶柱）
Dried shrimps	*har mai*	Xiā Mǐ	虾米
Dried sea cucumber	*hoi sum*	Haǐ Shēn	海参
Fried fish maw	*zao yu tou*	Chà Yú Dù	炸鱼肚
Shark's fins	*yu chee*	Yú Chì	鱼翅
Shrimp roe	*har tze*	Xiā Zi	虾子

FISH & SEAFOOD

Chinese carp	*lei yu*	Lǐ Yú	鲤鱼
Grouper	*sek pan*	Shí Bān Yú	石班鱼
Marble Gobe	*soon hock yu*	Sǔn Kè Yú	笋壳鱼
Oysters	*sung ho*	Shēng Háo	生蚝
Pomfret	*cheong yu*	Chāng Yú	鲳鱼
Snakehead fish	*sang yu*	Shēng Yú	生鱼
Sole	*pei mok yu*	Bǐ Mù Yú	比目鱼
Squid	*muk yu*	Mò Yú	墨鱼
Threadfin	*ma you*	Wǔ Yú	午鱼
Turtle meat	*shoi yu*	Shuǐ Yú	水鱼

MEAT & POULTRY

Barbecued pork	char siew	Chà Saō	叉烧
Chicken feet	kai keok	Jī Jiǎo	鸡脚
Chicken gizzards	kai sun	Jī Shèn	鸡肾
Chicken liver	kai yuen	Jī Gān	鸡干 (鸡胭)
Dried duck gizzards	larp ngarp sun	Là Yā Sèn	腊鸭肾
Fillet steak	gau lau	Niú Liǔ	牛柳
Fresh duck gizzards	ngarp sun	Xián Yā Sèn	鲜鸭肾
Dried pig's tendons	jue keok kan	Gān Zhū Jiǎo Jīn	干猪脚筋
Duck's webs	ngarp keok	Yā Zhǎng	鸭掌
Frog	teen kai	Tián Jī	田鸡
Lean pork	sao yok	Shòu Ròu	瘦肉
Mutton	yeung yok	Yáng Ròu	羊肉
Pig's brain	jue nou	Zhū Naǒ	猪脑
Pig's heart	jue sum	Zhū Xīn	猪心
Pig's kidney	jue yiew	Zhū Yaō	猪腰
Pig's liver	jue yuen	Zhū Gān	猪胭
Pig's spleen	jue wang lei	Zhū Héng Lì	猪横利
Pig's stomach	jue tou	Zhū Dù	猪肚
Pig's tail	jue mei	Zhū Wěi	猪尾
Pig's trotter (foreleg)	jue sou	Zhū Jiǎo	猪手
Pigeons	pak kap	Rǔ Gē	乳鸽
Pork loin	jue thai	Zhū Tí	猪蹄
Ox-tail	ngau mei	Niú Wěi	牛尾
Roasted duck	siew ngarp	Shaō Yā	烧鸭
Roasted pig's trotter	siew jue sau	Shaō Zhū Soǔ	烧猪手
Shin pork	jue jin	Zhū Zhǎn	猪蹍
Spare ribs	pai kuat	Pái Gù	排骨

INDEX